Narcissist Abuse Recovery

The Ultimate Guide for How to Understand, Cope, and Move on from Narcissism in Toxic Relationships

Jean Harrison & Melody Dixon

TABLE OF CONTENTS

Claim Your Free Gift: A **Powerful Blueprint** For Safely
ESCAPING The Hands Of Your Narcissist Abuser

As a way of saying thank you for your purchase, I'm offering a FREE guide that's *exclusive* to the readers of this book.

The **Narcissist Escape Blueprint** goes perfectly with this book to assist you in taking the next step of breaking free of your abuser and taking your life back into your own hands. We'll reveal:

- The critical system to have in place before leaving to ensure your safety
- A cost-free method for staying hidden to prevent your abuser from finding you.
- Essential arrangements you need to make to completely detach yourself from the narcissist!

To get your free Narcissist Escape Blueprint, visit: www.BonusGuides.com/escape

Introduction

One of the worst feelings of being a victim of narcissistic abuse is the idea that you're alone. You often become so isolated that you forget that many are struggling just as you are. Throughout this book, you will start to realize that you aren't alone at all; you are just another voice silenced by one who tried to be louder than you.

That's not going to happen anymore. Feel empowered and brave that you are here, ready to move on from one of the most challenging parts of your life. The purpose of this book is to help you recover from a narcissistic, abusive relationship.

You are someone, either male or female, who has been scarred by an abusive, narcissistic relationship. You must know what led you to this place of trauma and how to cope and move on to prevent an incident like this from ever happening again in the future, or educate others in a similar situation.

What you have been going through is not easy. It is confusing, traumatic, and scary. Far too often, you feel many negative emotions. Admitting what is happening can be scary, but accepting help from others is exactly what you will need to move forward. Even though the journey ahead may seem daunting, you are made to overcome.

The fears of what might happen when you leave could have passed through your head multiple times, making you stay even though you know you are being hurt. In this book, we will remind you of your worth and give you the power needed to stop this abusive cycle once and for all.

This book will provide you with practical techniques to break free from narcissistic relationships, recover from emotional scars, and protect yourself from predators in the future. Unfortunately, this might not have even been your first relationship that involved narcissistic abuse.

If you are not careful with how you approach the situation and move forward, you might find yourself back in the place that caused you so much pain from the beginning. You do not have to blame yourself because of the abuse that you experience, and you should never take responsibility for the hurt that you feel from others. Unfortunately, there are some things you might be doing, knowingly or not, that make you look more appealing to narcissistic abusers.

This book will provide you with the latest information and tips on how to cope and recover from narcissistic abuse. Some methods from the past remain helpful, but the more you discover about how the mind operates and the cycles that abusers follow, the easier it is to break the patterns and separate yourself from toxic situations.

Psychology can be confusing, and understanding why a brain operates the way it does can perplex even the experts. When you can look at the patterns among similar situations throughout various individuals, it is easier to discover the things that you need to do to end the abuse.

What Is Narcissism?

You might have heard of the term "narcissist" before in a context not discussing abuse. Maybe your friend refers to herself as a narcissist because she likes talking about herself and looking in the mirror. Maybe the guy that seems full of himself at the office gets called a narcissist by the other workers.

Most of the time, people assume that a narcissist is simply a person who is obsessed with themselves. If that's the case, it would seem that we are surrounded by narcissists. In reality, less than 10 out of 100 people will actually be considered narcissists.

Narcissism is clinically known as narcissistic personality disorder (NPD). It is seen more commonly in men, and it usually starts developing during someone's childhood. The challenging part of narcissistic personality disorder is that it's not easy to treat.

When you have depression or anxiety, which are common mental illnesses, you can treat them with therapy or medication, usually with the patient being an active participant. When it comes to an abusive personality disorder, narcissists are not likely to admit that they have a problem. They will, in fact, probably do as much as they can to deny the reality.

Narcissists can get into the heads of their victims only because they first got into their heads themselves. We think of narcissists as vain people who only care about themselves. They usually hate themselves, which is why they are so negative and abusive toward others.

Still, narcissists have many things in common, such feeling that they are better than others. They think they deserve to be treated better, and they consistently desire extra admiration even for things that are not particularly admirable. They do this as a defense mechanism because they usually have had experienced trauma that caused them to disassociate.

We aren't going to go over how to remedy a narcissist, however. Instead, we are going to focus on the people that narcissists have hurt along the way. Although narcissists are hurting themselves, victims of the abuse have much less of a say in what is happening to them, sometimes even none at all.

That's what's so hard about being the victim. You know that your abuser has gone through things in their life that have left scars, but that still doesn't give them the right to hurt you. That's the concept you have to remember most throughout this book.

Your abuser might have been abused themselves, but they have chosen to handle it differently. Now that you have been hurt, are you going to take it out on others? No, you have to work through your trauma and heal so that it doesn't spread to others or continue to cause you pain. Before we get to the healing, we first have to understand who the narcissist really is behind the words and faces they present to us.

Who Is the Narcissist?

When we start thinking of narcissists, maybe a popular figure pops into your head. Perhaps it's a political leader, actor, or musician. While any of these people might have a narcissistic personality disorder, what we have to focus on more is the fact that most abusers are very good at hiding their true identity.

Some narcissists will be your teachers, police officers, doctors, and the people making your food. They aren't always going to have a domineering glare and a devilish smile. In fact, they will usually have a warm smile and charming eyes that lure you in.

All narcissists have their own identities, and it is foolish to think that we can so easily categorize them. Once you get to know someone personally, it's easy to tell if that person is a narcissist. However, when you've just been introduced to someone through a mutual friend or you've just met someone online, you initially have no idea what that person might be capable of.

At this point, know whether a person is a narcissist. At first, they are everything you want in a friend, partner, or lover. They have it all, and you don't think anyone can compare. Then things will start to change quicker than you realize, and the narcissist is orchestrating.

We will get more into the details of what behaviors narcissists actually display and how that develops. We want to first emphasize the importance of knowing that not all narcissists look the same. If they did, we wouldn't have to worry so much about falling for their abusive tactics.

Psychopaths

People often throw the word "psycho" around when describing people. Psychopaths are also often compared to narcissists because they lack empathy, have manipulative behavioral tendencies, and are good at hiding their toxic personality traits.

The main difference is that narcissists are more likely to show their abusive behavior. They are sometimes shameless in getting attention and seeking validation. Psychopaths focus more on operating quietly. Outwardly, they have more emotional control, but much of what is inside is similar to a narcissist.

Sociopaths

Sociopaths share one thing in common with both psychopaths and narcissists — they lack empathy. The thing that sets them apart, however, is that they have very little emotional control. It will often show when they are angry, annoyed, and irritated. They are much more aggressive and far less calculated.
Sociopaths have trouble maintaining relationships as well. They can be rude and angry, often causing fights. Narcissists and psychopaths often cause fights, too, but they will make you think that it was all your fault.

Psychopaths do not feel shameful over their actions, but they will show you that they do feel shame. Narcissists sometimes feel remorse, but sociopaths rarely feel guilty for the things they do.

This can kind of help you to understand the spectrum of where a person might fall. All of them lack empathy and can be cold and calculated, but how they display remorse over this behavior can help you figure out who your abuser is so that you can best remedy the situation.

You might have been dealing with one of these personality disorders, as all symptoms will differ; but in this book, we are going to be focusing on narcissistic personality disorder.

What Causes Narcissism

We still can't figure out the exact cause of narcissistic behavior. While there are studies that might have certain conclusions based on predictions, we can only go so far when really digging into the minds of these abusers. For the most part, they will deny that they have any issue, so it's not as easy to find willing participants for NPD studies as it might be for those who are struggling with anxiety.

Sometimes narcissistic behavior develops in a certain parent-child relationship. Parents who were verbally abusive or negligent can lead to people having personality disorders later in life. It's important to remember that the "parents" of our abusers weren't always just their mom or dad. They might have had an older sibling, grandparent, uncle, or another figure in their life that was responsible for their development who also might have led to them having this disorder.

Origins of Narcissistic Behavior

All children display selfish tendencies, but through basic lessons, exposures in schools, and other childhood development factors, they grow out of it. When we are developing as children, we are focused on ourselves because that is how we understand the world. Our parents teach us that we need to share, hitting others isn't a proper way to express emotions, and being mean hurts other people's feelings. Children's needs must be met, or else, they will throw tantrums because they are displaying narcissistic tendencies. Kids don't care if their parents are talking on the phone; when they're hungry, they want to eat! They will get up in the middle of a movie and do what they want. They will take from babies, and display other irrational behavior because they simply don't know any better. Some children display behaviors like this more than others due to how they were raised, but for the most part, it's important to remember that this is natural for kids. We don't worry about it because we know that they will grow out of it. Their "selfish" personalities can't hurt others as much as adults displaying the same behavior would.

Narcissists still have those childish tendencies. This is because they weren't taught empathy correctly throughout those selfish years. They might not have been taught that being mean hurts others, and though we can see it more easily now as adults, they still don't fully grasp it because it wasn't a concept they learned as children. This is why treating narcissistic personality disorders is so challenging. Narcissists are usually those who have experienced trauma in their childhood. When we go through experiences like these, we usually carry the same emotional intelligence we had when we were the age of the trauma. A person who was neglected or verbally and physically abused as a child is one whose needs were not met. They likely experienced trauma at the level that stunted their development—meaning, they were already developing this personality before they even had the chance to be emotionally aware.

Socioeconomic Factors That Create Narcissism

It's unlikely that you would adopt a narcissistic personality disorder if you're a thirty-year-old man. It's something that has to be developed much earlier on to carry into adulthood. That being said, we also have to remember that there are factors that help to influence this type of behavior. Just look at many cases of abuse in Hollywood.

They often have teams of people who are aware of what is going on but don't confront the issue head-on. Many socioeconomic factors didn't cause narcissism, but aided in the development of this personality disorder, making the abuser less likely to realize that they're at fault. When things in our environment remind us that what we are experiencing is natural, of course, we are far less likely to disturb it.

Those who were brought up in a privileged home will be more at risk for developing narcissistic personality disorders, among other factors. Some socioeconomic changes that a person might go through, such as getting a better job, moving to a nicer neighborhood, getting a more expensive car, could all help inflate someone's sense of individualism and self-regard.

Not everyone that is wealthy is a narcissist, that's for sure. However, we do have to recognize how the false sense of power that comes with a higher socioeconomic class can make a narcissist more likely to have the sense that they are better than others.

Why Narcissists Abuse Emotionally and Psychologically

We've all likely experienced unfair situations that elicit a response such as "How can they do this to me?" These narcissists make us think that they love us. We get the sense that we are important to them and that we are their world.

Unfortunately, they are still abusing us, so we often look inward and ask ourselves what could we have possibly done wrong that led us to this punishment. While going through recovery, you need to this pattern of thinking. There is a reason why narcissists abuse emotionally and psychologically, and it certainly is not you.

The first reason why these narcissists abuse is because they don't have empathy. If you don't care about how another person feels, that certainly dictates the kind of person that you are. If a friend asked to hang out and you didn't want to, you'd just ignore the invite. If someone asked for help, it'd be easy to pretend that you didn't hear them. We have empathy, which makes us more likely to help people and less likely to feel comfortable with hurting them.

The biggest reason why abusers do what they do is that they don't understand whole object relations. This means that they don't see themselves and you grounded in reality. Instead, it's a mix of different emotions, delusions, and fantasies. They do not have the ability to look at you objectively.

When you see another person, you can identify traits that characterize them, like being funny, smart, and nice, while also recognizing that they can get annoying, are sometimes stubborn, and can be cranky in the morning. In most relationships, we see the good and the bad, and we take that other person as what they are, accepting all parts of their personality. This is because we understand whole object relations. A narcissist will not, so when they notice one of your bad qualities, they won't accept you. Only that one bad quality defines you, so they don't feel shameful, because they aren't thinking of the real person that you are.

Can Narcissists Feel Empathy?

Narcissists lack empathy because they weren't taught it — it's as simple as that. When we are presented with a threat, we have a fight or flight response, like all animals. If you went to scare a cat, they would either scratch you (fight) or run and hide under the couch (flee). We do the same thing and have been doing so since childhood.

A narcissist, as a child, will develop a flight response in the sense that they are hiding in their own minds. As a kid, you don't have the option to go somewhere else when being abused, and most of the time, you don't even know what abuse is. Instead of dealing with it in an emotionally healthy way, the child will flee to their minds and create a false sense of reality that makes it easier to deal with their abuser.

Empathy is also lacking because of their stunted emotional intelligence that didn't get the opportunity to develop when they were children. Emotional intelligence is the ability to be aware of your own as well as other people's feelings, and how or why they might react in a certain way. Narcissists were never taught this, and it can be harder to develop later in life, which is why they will often remain the way they are.

Narcissists also have trouble understanding *object constancy*. This is similar to whole object relations in that it deals with how you will react in difficult situations. When you get in a fight with loved ones, sometimes you might want to say something hurtful, but you hold back because you don't want to see them in pain. This is your object constancy. A narcissist never developed this skill, so when they are fighting with someone, they are going to do whatever it takes to make sure that the other person is hurt. They don't care if it was over even the smallest issue. When they are angry, that is the only thing that matters, and they are going to show their nasty side. When you have object constancy, you can manage the impulse to hurt the other person because you are rational. If we always voiced the thoughts that ran through our minds during a fight, we would have hurt a lot more people. We recognize those hurtful thoughts as unhealthy and choose not to say them. A narcissist will do the opposite.

The Rotten Core of Narcissistic Personality

As we previously mentioned, all narcissists are different. However, they all usually have certain things in common that make it easier to identify them. Though you might know your abuser well, you still want to recognize what traits they have that are narcissistic and which ones they might conceal. This way, you can be better equipped to deal with the different kinds of narcissists you encounter.

It's also important to see the signs and things your narcissist abuser does that you might not have realized were part of their abuse. While you might have thought you knew everything about the way they operate, you will be surprised at the other manipulation tactics you didn't realize you were a part of.

The Difference Between Healthy and Pathological Narcissism

Some people will think that self-love, admiration for one's character, or other signs that you might be "full of yourself" means that you are narcissistic. It's important to understand the difference. First and foremost, if someone's self-centered personality isn't hurting anyone, then they certainly are not a narcissist. There are many people who are incredibly confident, enjoy talking about themselves, and aren't afraid to show their true character. We can't label them as narcissists, and that's important to remember.

We still need to have traits that we like and a level of comfortability with ourselves. It is when you start to become delusional, paranoid, and angry with others because you feel like you are getting mistreated that you should be concerned. If a person fails to see reality, become hurtful for no reason, and refuse to listen to others, then these are the beginning signs that they may be suffering from narcissism.

Which Narcissist Are you Dealing With?

By coming to this book, it is clear that a narcissist is affecting your life. The first sign that you are dealing with a narcissist is in the way that they are making you feel. Someone who loves you will not make you feel bad, crazy, or guilty. Even if you might have done something wrong, belittling, shaming, and isolating are not healthy ways to handle matters.

The next thing you will have to look out for is how that narcissist is reacting to the things you are sharing with them. If you can't have a discussion without them getting angry, you should be worried. If they fail to see anything wrong with your relationship and even go so far as to blame you for any part of it, then it's likely that you have a narcissist on your hands.

The best way to rank your narcissist is to also look at the symptoms they have. Below, we will go through the traits of a narcissist. One or two might mean that they could have other mental health issues or personality disorders, but anything more than that and the level of how much you feel is true about them indicates that you're dealing with a narcissistic abuser.

Traits of Narcissists

Narcissist desire *attention* much more than other people. We all know those people that will do anything they can to be in the spotlight, but a narcissist takes that to an unhealthy level.

Even though they are abusive, narcissists can also be rather *charming.* They know how to make others feel loved and wanted, and they will always go out of their way to cover up any negative personality traits they might have. They will do whatever they can to fool the people around them into thinking that they are a charming person.

Pathological lying is very common for narcissistic abusers. They will do whatever they have to in order to get the people in their lives to believe the same reality as them. They will go as far as making up complete lies, but most of the time, they will exaggerate the truth so that it fits their image.

Narcissists will also have a sense of *entitlement*. They feel as though they know everything, and even when they are wrong, they will find a way to prove that they at least were justified for thinking the opposite. They think that they are more deserving than others and have a hard time sharing.

Arrogance is a common issue with narcissists. They don't think they have any flaws, and also have double standards when it comes to what behavior is right for them but wrong for others. They can also have trouble taking criticism.

Lack of empathy is the biggest one we've mentioned already, but also one of the most obvious signs of a narcissist. They might show that they care about you, but it's important to take note of how they treat others as well. If they are rude to service staff, other family members, and friends but completely kind to you, they might be a narcissist.

Control is incredibly important for narcissists, and they will do whatever it takes to get it. They look for control in the strangest way as well, and when they sense someone might be trying to take control over them, they will get incredibly defensive.

Manipulation is another warning sign for narcissists. They have spent their entire lives twisting reality to protect themselves from their own images of abuse, so of course, they are going to be very good at knowing just how to manipulate you.

Triangulation is a method narcissists use that involves pulling someone into the abuse cycle, maybe a friend, to team up against you in a fight. For instance, if you're both fighting, they might call a friend to join, saying, "Isn't she crazy?" or "I'm right, right?" and these situations can make you feel even more like you are in the wrong.

Inside the Distorted Mind of a Narcissist

Hopefully, by now you understand why you shouldn't take the term "narcissist" so lightly. They are so abusive. You probably knew this before getting into this book; however, it's important that we point out the misunderstandings people have had in the past around this kind of behavior.

In *the Diagnostic and Statistical Manual of Mental Disorders*, nine traits are used to determine if someone is a narcissist. These are the traits:

1. Grandiose sense of self
2. Has consistent fantasies of wealth and success
3. Believes they are more special than everyone else
4. Needs constant admiration
5. Sense of entitlement
6. Manipulative — takes advantage of others
7. Lacking empathy
8. Envious — and believes others are envious
9. Arrogant and willing to show it

We already discussed some of these traits but mostly in the sense of how you can identify them. We are going to dive deeper into these nine traits throughout the rest of this chapter, putting ourselves into the mind of the narcissist so we can fully grasp how and why they do the things they do to us. When you can start to make more sense of it, it becomes easier to heal from the trauma you've experienced.

We all have different fantasies when it comes to what we hope for the future, especially in terms of our success. When it comes to a person with narcissistic personality disorder, they will take the ideas of the future to the extreme, often fantasizing more intense scenarios than you would imagine.

Many narcissists will hide these fantasies because they are not often anywhere near the place they want to be in their life. They will fantasize about being wealthy, owning luxurious items, controlling others, and various scenarios where they are powerful in whatever sense they might measure such success. They do this because, as children, this was how they escaped abuse.

They couldn't find a new family, so when they started to experience the abuse once again, they would go to that place they created. Unfortunately, they stayed there into adulthood, and much of their sense of identity is built there. This identity and fantasy of success are all they know.

It is their comfort blanket. When their victims question their own delusions, they are forcing the narcissist to question that reality they created, which means they have to go back to their childhood and relive the trauma that helped them make this escape in the first place.

Narcissists are full of themselves — thinking that they're special and reminding themselves of that as they grew up. Someone who is truly confident and happy with who they are will accept their flaws.

They have learned to get past the qualities they didn't like about themselves and formed a strong identity that they operate on. Individuals that are narcissists deny their flaws. They don't know how to take in the good and process it in a healthy way, making it hard to accept that they have any flaws at all.

Narcissists know how to validate themselves. They will often break other people down in their minds, especially if they think that others are jealous of them and envious of the things that they have.
Most of the time, narcissists will have these feelings of envy themselves, but they will mask it by pointing fingers at the other person. Because of the delusions they've built in their minds and the feeling of being better than others, they've formed a sense of

entitlement.

How to Learn the Language of Narcissists

There is nothing more confusing than trying to reason or argue with a narcissist. They will often tell you lies, manipulate you, and make you believe something that isn't true. They are so good at lying and do so often to the point that you can't tell what the truth is anymore.

They will also present challenges in communication because often, you cannot read their body language or facial expressions very well. They might be smiling while they're arguing, or look annoyed even when they are telling you that they're fine.
This happens because they don't always have the control needed to manage reactions properly or they might be trying to get more attention from you.

For narcissistic abusers that do not use physical violence, their biggest weapon is their language. The way they talk to you is the only way that they can ensure that they're hurting you.

If we can learn to understand the language of narcissists, it will be a lot easier to brush them off when they're picking a fight or avoid letting their words hurt us when they are breaking us down. Know first, that when speaking to a narcissist, they aren't necessarily lying, but they are likely fabricating the truth. They aren't always intentionally doing this either. They might be recounting a story about how they went to the store, and the cashier was so rude to them that it ruined their day.

In reality, they were just as rude to the cashier, and it was a fight that could have been prevented had both parties just kept their cool. However, narcissists always think that it's the other person's fault because they don't have the ability to self-reflect and see what they might have contributed.

In a sense, they are not lying to you when they tell you this because that is exactly what they think the truth is. However, if you're going to understand that narcissists have a different kind of language than you, then it's important to see that they are only telling their side of the story. Most people will do this.

It's not often that when you're in a heated situation, you share the other person's side as well. With narcissists, they will refuse to see reality even if you bring it up, and they won't try to process that situation and grow from it. Instead, they will spend the next few days replaying the circumstance to their favor, reiterating in their own minds that they didn't do anything wrong.

How They Think

Once you understand how narcissists communicate with you, it will become much easier to see how they think. This is going to help you deal with them if you have to keep in contact and mend the wounds left from all the hurtful things they've said and done.

Narcissists tend to think arrogantly, such as: "I love myself and so does everyone else. It's hard to picture someone who doesn't love me." They are deeply insecure, but they don't realize it. If you are feeling insecure (maybe with the way you look), before you go to a party, you might put on nicer clothes, wear extra makeup, or do something else to boost your confidence. If a narcissist is feeling self-conscious, they are just going to go to that party and make fun of others to distract themselves from the fact that they have low self-esteem.

If they were aware of what was going on, they could take a step back and think about why they feel the need to deflect and resolve their issue by trying to boost their confidence. Instead, they distract their minds from feelings of insecurity, make someone else look bad to take the pressure off themselves, but still make jokes so that they get attention and validation from others. Not all narcissists are funny, either. Someone might straight up make a rude comment, like, "What were you thinking when you put that shirt on?"

A narcissist might think, "What would these people do without me? I need to do everything around here." We all might have had thoughts like this. If you're a parent, you might look at chores as your way of "doing everything." However, we usually have a grounding moment where we remember that although we have an important role, we aren't the only ones capable of fulfilling it. We help other people, but they do not depend on us.

Narcissists fully believe that others will depend on them. They aren't always wrong, but it is usually because they've conditioned those around them to be dependent. They've built themselves up to a point where they have managed to convince others of their grandiosity, making it hard for them to see that, in reality, others would survive just fine without them.

The Narcissist's False Self and True Self

Narcissists have two different identities. Whether they are aware of it or not is something that really only they will know. Rarely will a narcissist tell you that they are a narcissist and fully aware of it, unless they are in active recovery.

Most of the time, they will be completely delusional and defensive that there's something wrong with them. This is why it's important for us to know the distinction between a narcissist's false self and true self.

Their false self is what the narcissist was able to construct, usually in defense of their abuse. We keep discussing that the narcissist has been abused, but there are some cases where narcissist developed their personalities for other reasons, so that's also important to understand. However, there is still an event that happened in their life that caused them to create this false self. Knowing this can help you read your narcissist abuser better. Therefore, understand that there was likely something that caused this, and it's not because they were just born a villain.

The false self is based on all nine traits that we discussed previously. These all formed in order to create some kind of "superhero" in the narcissist's head, in the sense that they don't have many flaws. The problem with this false self is that it is unstable.

All humans are flawed, and we all have traits that might need working on. The false self doesn't need any work, and the narcissist isn't afraid to tell you this. That is why narcissists go through cycles. They don't care about improving. They only have the determination to protect that false self.

The real self is what lies underneath the narcissist's delusions. All the personality traits that they actually have, along with the things that they might need to work on and improve, are hidden in the true self.

This is what we are more aware of. At first, when building the relationship, you might have seen this false self. You could have fallen for the façade and enjoyed the grandiosity that they so often displayed. However, as time goes on and the abuse starts, the real self will emerge, and it can get ugly. Since the narcissist devotes their life to protecting this false self, few people can really see through it and will instead fall for what they see on the outside. It's only when the narcissist is vulnerable (in a place where they aren't being attacked but their false self is) that they will start the abuse cycle.

When you start voicing opinions in the relationship, that's when things might get more challenging. When we're with new people, we often overlook the things they do that bother us and go through a "smitten" phase, where we only care about having fun with the other person.

Then, when the fun starts to fade, reality will set in — but not for the narcissist. You start to question their false self, pointing out the things they do that you don't like or letting them know when they might have hurt you.

The Way a Narcissist Can Get Inside Your Head

Gaslighting is the most common way that a narcissist or any verbal abuser for that matter will get inside your head. Gaslighting involves making you feel as though your "side of the story" is wrong. They will often call you crazy, say that you're being too emotional, or tell you that you are remembering things wrong. Rather than arguing with you, they will just completely dismiss anything that you're saying and make you think that you are crazy.

Sometimes, people are too emotional. They might have misunderstood a situation or were being especially sensitive to what someone said. That doesn't matter though. If a person is hurt, they are hurt. The other member of the relationship needs to be aware of this. Rather than saying something rational, such as, "I never meant to hurt you, and I am so sorry that I caused you to feel that way. I hope you know that the comment was not meant to be taken the wrong way," a narcissist will say, "You're absolutely insane. I never said anything remotely close to that, and you are being way too dramatic."

To make matters worse, they will use triangulation, as we mentioned previously. This is most commonly seen in relationships with couples, with the other person only telling their side of the story to a close friend or family member. They get inside that other person's head and only share their side of the story so that the other person can validate them and be their "backup."

Looking to others for help with relationship issues is fine in some situations, but not when you are only sharing one side of the story and inflating it so that you look innocent. This is what a narcissist will do.

The Shame/Grandiosity Continuum

This is what the narcissist uses to crush your self-esteem and fool you into feeling inferior. There is a continuum that exists between self-contempt and state of contempt of others. On one end, you are feeling as though you aren't good enough.

On the other, you feel as though you have no boundaries. Usually, in a narcissistic relationship, one person will be on one end, and the other on the opposite. A healthy relationship involves two people in the middle, in a mutual place of love and acceptance for each other.

Mind Control and Manipulation

A narcissist uses mind control and manipulation to break down and rebuild your identity for the purpose of subjugation. They will do whatever they have to in order to get in your head and make you feel inferior. The most common forms of manipulation are:

1. Targeting your flaws
2. Pointing out insecurities
3. False praise

All these will either get you on the side of the manipulator or make you feel so low that you believe everything they say. They can make you feel low to a point where you can't trust your own feelings anymore.

A Short message from the Author:

Hey, are you enjoying the book? I'd love to hear your thoughts!

Many readers do not know how hard reviews are to come by, and how much they help an author.

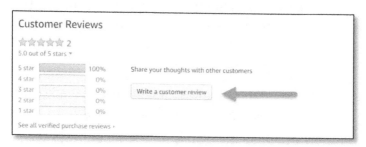

I would be incredibly grateful if you could take just 60 seconds to write a brief review on Amazon, even if it's just a few sentences!

To leave a brief review, please visit:
www.**TitleRatings.com/narcissist**

Thank you for taking the time to share your thoughts!

Your review will genuinely make a difference for me and help gain exposure for my work.

Why You Keep Attracting Narcissists

Narcissists know that they can't simply find just anyone to fall under their spell. There are plenty of people out there who are going to be more aware of what they're up to, especially another narcissist. If you get two people with NPD in a room together, it's not going to be pretty.

Oftentimes, family members might display these kinds of personalities, which is why you might be part of an entirely dysfunctional family or one that always seems to be fighting. There are also many narcissist enablers out there that can make it easier for narcissists to operate the way they do. Narcissists will keep these enablers by their side throughout the various cycles of abuse.

Narcissists are in a constant need of having a victim as well. If they do not, then they will start to act anxiously, erratically, and flustered. This is why it can be so hard to leave. They worked so hard to condition you a certain way that they don't want to have to go over those processes again with another person.

We often wonder what it might have been that caused the narcissist to "choose us." I often felt that I was burdened for loving someone that could be a narcissist. I would think to myself how easier life would have been if I had fallen in love with someone else. However, it's not completely by chance. The narcissist has specific targets in mind.

Narcissists will look for people who don't seem to have a strong support system. They might find lonely people or those who don't have many friends. They do this because they know it will be easier to make those people depend on them.

This isn't to say that you don't have anyone who loves you; it's just that the narcissist sees that they can easily take you from your social situation to either isolate you or turn you against your loved ones. Aside from this, there are many other traits that the narcissist might have identified in you that we will discuss throughout the rest of the chapter.

Those Attracted to Narcissists

In no way should you feel shameful for having fallen into a relationship with a narcissist. Though there are some traits you might have in common with other people that make you more attracted to narcissists, this isn't something that we should break ourselves down over. Instead, we need to focus on recognizing this reality and improving from it, making us the best versions of ourselves that we can be.

It's important to remember that often, a narcissist will choose you because they see your empathy. You are a kind and caring person that the narcissist is going to want to take from. They will see your generosity and kind spirit as one that they can appropriate for themselves. They want to get the attention and care that you have inside of you, and they want to deplete you of it. A lot of times, narcissists will succeed, and then they will move on to their next target.

Traits of Their Targets

Victims of narcissists are just as different from the narcissists themselves. Just because you have suffered abuse doesn't mean that you are all the same, any less worthy, or lacking value. It is, however, important to note similar traits among narcissistic victims so that you can understand why you are being targeted and be better prepared to protect yourself against these energy vampires.

No matter how intelligent, outgoing, or kind a person is, a narcissist will still be able to see their insecurities, and they will use them to their advantage. Anyone displaying low self-esteem, insecurity, or self-consciousness will be a target for a narcissist. This is because narcissists will see that as a weakness. They see a "hole in the wall" where they can tear you down and make you feel even more insecure than you already are.

If you are insecure, in no way, shape, or form does it mean that you are "weak." That is what a lot of people might have the misconception about when it comes to those that have been abused by narcissists. Most victims are the opposite, in fact. They have a sense of independence, responsibility, and success that narcissists feel they can take from.

They don't want someone who is "needy." They want someone that is self-sufficient because they aren't looking to take care of other people. They might think they are better than others, but that child that was hurt inside of them still wants someone that will take care of them. They want someone kind and empathetic.

The narcissist will often see this independence in you and look for ways to complement it. They will like that you can take care of yourself, and they will praise you for being so empathetic and kind. As time goes on, they will start to break your spirit, pulling from your insecurities. Some might believe this is because they are jealous, and others simply think it's the way for narcissists to get what they want from you. The type of people that narcissists will commonly go after is discussed in the following section.

Codependents

A codependent is a person who requires another individual to take care of. Some people think codependent just means hating being lonely and wanting to have someone close to you. In reality, codependency involves the codependent (a person who wants to take care of others) and the dependent (a person who gets taken care of).

You will often see this in parents that might be overprotective to the point that they act irrationally. This is because they have avoided taking care of themselves for so long that they don't know who they are if they aren't caring for others. A narcissist is a person who needs something. A narcissist needs to be taken care of, to be validated. The codependent has something to give— care and validation. The two will match perfectly with each other. The codependent will ignore their needs, usually because they don't want to have to confront their own traumas. They will take care of the narcissist even though they might feel like the narcissist is the one who is in control.

This relationship feels great at first. The codependent feels like they have a purpose. They see this damaged person (the narcissist) and think that they can take care of them. They do this because it is often easier to take care of other people than to take care of themselves. The narcissist thinks that they finally found the person to take care of them, not concerned that the codependent might be too preoccupied with being the caretaker.

The codependent is always under the power of the other person even though they think they are in charge. They might be the one taking care of the other person, but they need to do that to fulfill themselves. The narcissist will be in control completely, but the codependent doesn't realize that because they are used to this false illusion of control.

This is a common relationship seen in heteronormative romantic relationships. There is usually a brooding man. Maybe he's tougher, more emotionally closed off, or seemingly stoic. Then there is a powerful woman who knows how to take care of herself and her man.

Only in this case, she's really taking care of him because that is her identity — to follow him. He takes advantage of her generosity and uses her. She thinks that she is helping him, that she could be "saving" him, but really, he is just using this need to fulfill his own selfish intentions.

Empaths and Highly Sensitive People

We have talked a lot about empathy throughout this book, but the term "empath" is referring to someone different. An empath is a person who feels emotions more deeply than others. They can tell when a person might be upset better than the average person and potentially better than the upset person themselves. Some people believe that there might be metaphysical aspects behind those that call themselves empaths.

For science-based individuals, an empath can be interchanged with the term "highly sensitive person," or HSP. Narcissists love both HSPs and empaths because they are filled with empathy, something that the narcissist completely lacks. Both HSPs and empaths have been called sensitive people in their lives, and there's a high chance that they have been gaslighted as well.

Since the narcissist needs constant admiration and validation, they will look to these HSPs, who have plenty to offer. The HSP can usually tell that the narcissist has deeper hurt under what they are showing, but they won't always be aware of the relationship that is going on. They will often fall victim to the narcissist, sometimes getting their high level of empathy and bright spirit crushed along the way.

How You Qualify as a Target

It's not like those that fall victim to narcissists are looking for this kind of relationship. For the most part, it happens fast and without them realizing exactly what's going on. You can get so lost in the relationship that even when your closest friends or family members tell you that they're worried about this narcissistic person, you don't listen whatsoever.

Once you've escaped the abuse cycle, it's easy to beat yourself up over it. You might think that you were foolish to have fallen into this relationship or that you played a big part in your abuse. You have to remember though, that hurting yourself over what happened isn't going to help you move forward. Narcissists are skilled people, and there are ways that you unwittingly qualified yourself as a target of the narcissists. It could be that you possess something that makes you a desirable option to the narcissist. Maybe it's your job, lifestyle, or generosity. Whatever successful aspect of your life it may be, it's what the narcissist picks out to destroy.

If a narcissist is meeting your family, they might show a lot of joy and interest at first. They will build up their excitement and get you feeling confident about meeting them. Then there will be a rapid switch where they might end up mocking or belittling your family, even being passively aggressive toward them when you meet.

They do this to give you the illusion that they were perfect in the scenario but *your family* was the one that destroyed their excitement. This will come in handy later when they try to isolate you from your close friends and family in order to gain full control over you.

What Are Your Personal Traps

It's important to understand and identify your personal traps so that you can avoid falling prey to the narcissist. To do this, first identify what sets you apart from others. There has to be something that makes you unique. It could be your energetic personality, your commitment to helping others, or even simply the amount of people in your life that love you.

Next, look at your level of vulnerability. Do you share with others your feelings of insecurity? Do you have weaknesses that you aren't afraid to hide? This isn't a bad thing, but the narcissist might be able to easily pick up on them and use them to their advantage.

Finally, do you have codependent traits? Do you have a need to help others to the point where you are ignoring your own needs? If you are a giving person that never expects anything back and isn't concerned about mutual return in some relationships, then the narcissist can use this to their advantage as well.

What Does they Want from You?

The narcissist wants validation. They want to feel like they are right and that they aren't necessarily doing anything wrong. The narcissist is looking at you to help them feel safe. At the same time, they are so frightened that you are going to leave, that you will take that safety with you. They need to destroy your confidence, self-esteem, and all that you have to offer so that you won't leave them.

The narcissist will convince you that you don't have anything worthy to offer but that they love you in spite of that so that you will stay with them because you don't think you will have any worth elsewhere. The narcissist will gaslight you to make you feel crazy and like your emotions are out of control.

The narcissist will change your pattern of thinking so that you will believe what they say, and you might even form narcissistic tendencies yourself from being with them for too long. They are desperately looking for love. They don't consciously think this, but they are hoping to break everyone down around them to the point that they are surrounded by people who think highly of them.

Only then will the narcissist, in their mind at least, be satisfied. They want that security in the form of people who will love and support them, and they believe that the only way to build this network is to break people down, making them loyal emotional servants that will continually offer them empathy and support.

The Effects of Narcissism

We have all had relationships with people who maybe weren't the best for us. They might have been bad influences, negative thinkers, or people that we simply didn't vibe with. The difference between a person you don't get along with and a person who will emotionally manipulate you is that the manipulator is trying to change the way that you think.

They get inside your head and plant ideas that only they believe to be true so that they can convince you to believe them as well. It is a toxic pattern that can be inescapable. If you were told every day that if you went outside, you would die, you would start to believe this and become fearful of the outside world even after being told that it was a lie!

Narcissists put us through terrible things when we're with them, but unfortunately, the abuse doesn't stop there. They will continue to hurt us in a pattern that destroys our identity even if we are miles away from them. The following sections are the behaviors a narcissist will instill in us and what will continue even long after the abuse has ended. It is important to recognize these so that we're aware that they were put there by the narcissist, making it easier to get over them in the end.

Toxic Shame

Narcissists love to create shame in their victims. They will tell them often that they should feel guilty, embarrassed, and shameful over the things that they might have done. They don't care if this makes us feel terrible; they need to create this shame to make us question ourselves. Then we question why we would even deserve someone better than the narcissist, making it harder to leave.

A Dissociated Mind

Just like a child will create an image in their head to escape to during abuse, so will the victims of the narcissist. A narcissistic abuse survivor is likely very good at dissociating. This involves our brain detaching from the scenario, like if you were "zoning out" or "lost in space." We do this so that we can shut out the abuse. For instance, if you were driving in a car with the narcissist, they might start telling you all the things that are wrong with you or what you did that you shouldn't have done. A dissociated mind will look out the window, ignoring what they're saying on one level while still taking it in subconsciously. You will not stand up for yourself because it's just easier to stay quiet. There's no point in fighting back, and sometimes you don't know how, so instead, you will focus on dissociating.

A Weakened Ego

Your identity can be stripped from you because of the narcissistic abuse. The abuser can make you feel as though you are a bad person, you did something wrong, and that you have made too many mistakes. The moment you believe that, your ego becomes weakened.

Low Self-Esteem and Inferiority

It's clear to see how narcissists will induce low self-esteem in their victims, which can leave them feeling insecure and inferior even long after the abuser is gone. When you are feeling confident, you might still hear the abuser in the back of your head, thinking only of what they would say in a situation. It is important to know just how inferior they make you feel so that you can combat this negative self-talk when it happens.

The narcissist never makes you feel good enough. You will always be left feeling like you have done something wrong and that you should be shameful over the normal human emotions you experience. Moving forward, do not let yourself think like this anymore. It won't happen overnight, but each time you start to feel inferior, remember that it was the narcissistic abuse that told you to feel this way.

Signs of an Abusive Narcissistic Relationship

We've discussed a lot about the narcissistic abuser traits. However, it's important that we actually start to focus on what a narcissistic relationship looks like. The most common behaviors you will experience in a narcissistic relationship are gaslighting, triangulation, sabotage, projection, stonewalling, isolation, and many other personality disorder traits that leave you trapped in a cycle of abuse.

After going through some of these experiences, there may be moments when you begin struggling with PTSD, or complex PTSD if it were a longer-term relationship when you were younger, like through narcissistic parents. This kind of abuse isn't going to be overcome easily, but you will get past it. Time is the best healer, and it's important to make sure that you are giving that to yourself.

Although it can be easy sometimes to see signs in a narcissistic relationship, we don't always realize the abuse that's happening to us. Often, the other person will make us feel crazy, and we can end up having a hard time trusting our judgments and opinions in the long term. You might even develop anxiety and depression because of this, in addition to challenging flashbacks that could be triggered by other stressful situations.

The best way to get over this abuse cycle is to be aware of all the signs that made the relationship narcissistic. This way, you can immediately recognize a toxic relationship if the future. Also, there are some cases in which the abuser might recognize what has happened, and the two can actively work together to find a resolution.

However, this is rare, as manipulators won't admit what they're doing, and even if they do, that might just be yet another manipulation tactic. However, the more equipped you are with the knowledge of everything that is involved in this abusive behavior, the easier it will be for you to move past this and get to a place where you can heal, feel safe, and be happy.

Red Flags of Abusive Behavior and Covert Manipulation Tactics

The first red flag that you are going to notice is projection. This is when the other person is going to place their feelings of insecurity onto you. You might make a slight joke, but they will take great offense, making you feel guilty about even thinking it in the first place. Afterward, they are going to shame you and always remind you of that time you made them feel bad.

They are also going to make you feel bad because of their own insecurities. They will make you feel like you are dumb, haven't accomplished anything, or simply can't do anything right. That is a big one for narcissistic abusers. They will always be ready to point out your minor incompetence to make you feel as worthless as possible.

Another red flag is avoidance of emotions, from you at least. When they make you feel silly for crying or shame you for having any emotion at all, this is going to be another big sign that you're dealing with a narcissist. They will make you feel weak for having any feeling at all. They will laugh at you if you're being "too sensitive," and will do whatever it takes to dismiss your feelings so they don't have to admit that they might have been hurtful and flawed in any way.

They are going to have a very murky past as well. They might tell you one story about their childhood that makes it seem as though they were in a terrible situation, but then when the time calls for it, they will brag to others about all the great things they did as a kid. Whatever the truth is, it doesn't always matter; what matters is what they choose to tell you that will make you start to question why their past is so fragmented. Most of the time, narcissists aren't going to admit that they experienced abuse either. They might say things that seemed abusive, but if you were to bring that up, they would likely get angry and dismissive.

This seems counterintuitive, but narcissists will often put you on the pedestal. You might not think that a person who is obsessing over you is a narcissist because our preconceived notions tell us that a narcissist is a different kind of person. However, they do this so that they can make you feel incredibly unique at first. That way, you fall under their good graces, and it will be easier for them to dismiss you later on.

At the same time, they think that if they are surrounded by perfect people, they might experience some of those good qualities as well. What will end up happening, however, is that the narcissist will idolize you to the point where reality is lost, and they fail to see your flaws. Then, when you become flawed, it will go against their idealizations, breaking down some of the created realities they managed to fabricate and causing them to become incredibly upset.

Narcissists need to be in control at all times. They are very concerned with making sure that they are in charge and that everyone around them is aware of that. At the same time, they won't always do so in an authoritative way. If they take charge at first, they aren't going to make it seem obvious that they are controlling. Instead, they might ask you to lead so that when something goes wrong, they can say things like, "If I did it, none of this would be happening." Parents will often do this with their children as well if they have narcissistic personality disorders. They will ask them to do a very challenging task that they know the child is incapable of completing, and then come in to save the day when their child ultimately fails, as they had planned from the beginning.

Narcissists will get very upset when they don't get their way. They'll even go as far as throwing mini "tantrums" when other people are getting the attention they "deserve." For example, you might go to your friend's birthday party, where you'll likely be giving them more attention than your narcissistic partner. As a result, your partner might act out. Maybe they feel sick, start to drink too much, get in a fight, or do whatever else they have to in order to get your attention back.

Anytime you feel concerned about approaching your partner, parent, or whoever else you might be involved with in a narcissistic relationship, you have to take into consideration that it might be abusive. Relationships should be open in the sense that there is trust and honesty so that you aren't afraid to approach the other person with your feelings. If you're scared to say something to your partner as you would be to your teacher or your boss, it's time to do some serious evaluation of this relationship.

Subtle Signs Many Survivors Don't Catch in the Early Stages of Dating a Narcissist

While there are obvious signs of narcissistic abuse, it's necessary to recognize the subtler signs that not everyone will detect at first. The less you are aware, the easier it will be to start a potentially toxic relationship. At the very least, you can confront people about this behavior in the beginning and see how they react, knowing that if they can't talk about their emotions at the start, they certainly won't be able to later on.

A subtle sign to look for is narcissists will feel like they are owed something. When you don't text back, when you don't go home with them on the first date, or even if the waiter forgets to bring their extra side of fries, they will at first be upset and question what they did to deserve this unfair treatment. Later down the line, they can get angry even to the point of being aggressive.

Narcissists also don't follow the rules. Everyone has been attracted to a bad boy, but we're not talking about stealing cars or fighting. We mean that they won't be courteous to others, like waiting their turn for a table at a restaurant or standing in line at the bank. They will do whatever they can to break the rules set in place but not in a sexy, dangerous kind of style — more like a kindergartener that is eager to get more than the rest of their classmates.

You won't ever be able to criticize, coach, lecture, or advise a narcissist. They already know it all. It is common for people to not like to be told what to do, but a narcissist takes it to an extreme level. You might simply tell them, "Your shoe is untied," only for them to give a five-minute response in defense of this minor slip-up, potentially blaming it on someone else. No matter how small the occurrence, those that are narcissistic will have no interest in listening to any sort of advice.

Narcissists have no regard for other people's time, and there will certainly be double standards in place. If something more interesting comes up, they will cancel on you without feeling guilty, even if it's five minutes before your date was scheduled. If you did the same thing to them, however, they would not handle it so well. Even if you canceled a whole week in advance, they might have an outburst or ignore you altogether, because they take it as an attack against their character.

A narcissist is incredibly impatient as well. They will tap their feet, clear their throat, nod their head, and roll their eyes as a sign that they want you to hurry up. They have no problem sitting on the couch all day while doing nothing, but as soon as they ask you to do a certain task, they expect it to be done within seconds. The world operates according to their clock.

The Narcissistic Abuse Cycle

Humans love patterns, traditions, habits, and other repeated cycles they can depend on. These all give us a sense of security. When you go to work from nine to five, five days a week, you have job security. People will order the same thing at a restaurant every time they go because they know they will like it. We seek this security in many ways, as do narcissists. Unfortunately, they also take their victims through a pattern — the abuse cycle.

It's important to recognize this pattern so that you can break it. Doing this could potentially even help your abuser, though that should not be your primary goal. You might find that you are also comfortable with this cycle. Though you might have to struggle with the abuse, it can still provide the dependence that some of us are craving so desperately in our lives.

Although it's wrong, the cycle of abuse can be comforting because it is something that you depend on. Know that you deserve so much more than this cycle and that you have to get out of this abusive loop as soon as you can. The more you go through it, the harder it will be to break free from it.

Idealize

The first step of this cycle is the narcissist makes you feel special. This is why it's hard to catch, as all relationships should be founded on making the other person feel important, validated, and loved. A narcissist will take this to the extreme. They will make you think you are soulmates, try to rush the relationship, and let you know that you are unlike anyone else they have ever been with before. This is their way of getting you hooked and locked in.

Devalue

After they've reeled you in, they will start to let their false self-crumble and show their true character. They will likely be passive aggressive at first by making jokes about your character that they shrug off by simply saying that they are a sarcastic person. You might notice that they are laughing often but usually with you as the butt of the joke. All relationships have moments of teasing, but the devaluing will start to grow. After a while, there won't be any jokes; instead, it will be full-blown verbal abuse, much like what we mentioned in the previous chapters.

Discard

This might be the final phase for some narcissistic abuse cycles. The abuser will have destroyed you, broken you down, and made you feel awful about yourself. They will have lowered your self-esteem to the point that you're not even the same person anymore.

Once they have done this, they might grow bored with you and discard you, moving on to the next victim. This is the phase when they will say the most hurtful things to you, letting you know that you have no value, no friends, and no worth. They no longer see anything they can take from you, so they won't be afraid to let the nastiest things come out of their mouth.

Destroy

For some, the last phase comes to this. However, the narcissist might not fully be done with you. They might realize that you still have something left for them to take or that letting you go and starting over with someone new would be a burden. This is when they will try to bring you back up, remind you that you need them, and let you know that they aren't going to hurt you anymore.

This is the part of the cycle that pulls people who almost escaped right back in. They will tell you how sorry they are, how they didn't mean any of it, and how much they love you. How good it feels to hear this as the victim! The person that you idolized, that person that was your world, the person that just hurt you worse than ever. Now, they are sorry! They admit that they were wrong. You think things will get better, just as they were in the very first idealized state. Only now, they are going to take you right back through that cycle. They have managed to destroy who you are, and now have you wrapped around their finger.

Hoover

Hoovering is another technique that many people use to describe how a narcissist pulls their victims back into the relationship. It was given that name because of the vacuum and the powerful way that it can suck up dirt and grime.

If you managed to escape during any of the phases before being destroyed, then you will likely experience this phase. First, the narcissist will call you, text, write letters, send flowers, and give subtle communication after a separated period. As soon as you respond, the cycle starts all over again, with the abuser idealizing you once more.

The Obstacles That Keep You Trapped in a Cycle of Narcissistic Abuse

We sometimes put ourselves in unhealthy relationships because we are like children who want to find resolve and satisfaction. Because of this, many people will end up suffering from the need to fulfill those childlike desires, resulting in irrational behavior and making decisions that are not in their best interest, i.e., staying in an abusive relationship. These next four sections are all the things that narcissists do that will keep us trapped in the abusive relationship. These are the tactics that they use in the destruction and hoovering phases to make sure that once the cycle ended the first time, you're going to be there to go through it again and again and again.

The Psychological Cage

As a victim of abuse, you may have found yourself in a psychological cage before that you were placed in by your abuser. If we were ever to have complete control over our enemies, we'd have them locked away, leaving them waiting for our beck and call. However, that's illegal, so narcissists find a way of creating a psychological cage to keep their victims trapped. They have created a world where you are nothing and have no value without them.

You helped to create the cage as well, as it is protecting you. While it's what is holding you back, keeping you locked away from your friends, special events, and doing the things you once enjoyed, it also keeps you away from your abuser. You can hide, in a sort of dissociative state, away from the world, in the psychological cage.

Love Starvation / **Love Bombing**

Just like many narcissists are abuse victims, many of us have experienced forms of abuse as well. Perhaps your parents were abusers, or maybe you were bullied in school. Either way, we likely went through a period of love starvation, a time when we were emotionally hungry and desired human affection. Then the narcissist came in and love-bombed us during the idealization phase. Though it's only one part of the cycle, they gave us so much love that it keeps us coming back for more. It might have just been the first month in a year-long relationship since you've experienced this love-bombing, but those that have been starved of passion in the past will wait out the cycle, hoping to get a taste of all that affection once again.

Low Shame Tolerance / Shamelessness

A narcissist can destroy your identity so that you will have a pretty low shame tolerance. Some people are even shameless because they no longer care what anyone thinks but their abuser. Friends and family may warn you that you are being abused, but you aren't ashamed of the relationship, so you ignore them and stay. You might have gotten into a fight with them in public or at a social gathering, but the shamelessness has caused you not to care what anyone else thinks and focus only on how your abuser is reacting.

Even though your narcissistic abuser yells at you in front of a group of people, you still go running to them because they have given you such a low shame tolerance. This keeps us around because we don't listen to others who inform us of these warning signs. We don't have a healthy perception of relationships, so instead, we run to them.

Guilt and Conditioning

The narcissist is going to do whatever they have to in order to make you feel guilty. They have conditioned you to think that you are a bad person and they are good. You don't matter, and they do. If you do something wrong to them, they will make you feel terrible about it long after that time has ended. If they do something terrible to you, then you still feel guilty for bringing it up and making them feel bad about it.

The Motives behind Narcissistic Abuse

All this seems so exhausting! When looking at how a narcissist acts, we can start to become shocked. Why go through all that when they can simply get love in other ways? There are plenty of loving relationships in the world where both people benefit and where their thoughts and opinions are easily shared. Unfortunately, the narcissist doesn't know this. They have a completely warped perspective on reality and only think negatively in a way that suits them the most.

Why They Feed Off Other People

Narcissists lack empathy, which usually means that they are unaware of their emotions. They still get sad and angry, and those feelings are valid, but they don't know what those emotions are or how to manage them properly. What will end up happening is they decide to look to other people in a desperate attempt at understanding them.

We still don't know everything about narcissists on a scientific level, but what we can predict is that they are desperately reaching out to other people in an attempt to understand emotions and feelings. They will do this in dangerous ways, by getting the most out of us and hoping for emotional reactions that will satisfy the urges that they don't fully understand. They are desperate for love, and if they make another person desperate enough, they might be able to have them stick around, giving them the false sense that they are loved.

Why Abused Survivors Stay

It can seem so perplexing to come up with reasons why survivors stay with narcissists long after the incidents of abuse occur. As an outsider to other abusive relationships, you wonder, "How can they stay?" When you look at other relationships after being in a loving one yourself, it is so surprising to think of a time when you let yourself be in an abusive relationship. There are reasons, however, and it's not your fault! Don't feel sorry and shameful, as you were manipulated into this. However, moving forward, make sure you are aware of why it was that you stayed with this narcissist so that you don't have to worry about ever going back.

One of the biggest reasons that a victim stays with a narcissist, or with any abuser for that matter, is that they are scared. They don't know what is going to happen when it comes time for them to leave. They are afraid of exiting that cycle because, though challenging, it still provided them with a sense of security. It was something that they were always able to rely on. The narcissist made you think you can't survive without them, so of course, you're going to be scared of what happens when it's time to leave.

After that, they are also afraid of how the abuser is going to retaliate. They might have shared personal information with them, perhaps a nude photograph or video, a secret of their sexual orientation or identity, or perhaps even a crime. They might be afraid that the abuser is going to use any of this secretive information shared against them.

Abusers are also afraid simply because of their culture. If you are raised in a Christian household that is against divorce, you might end up staying in this relationship even though it's toxic, all because of the strict views you had growing up.

People will also stay because of financial and family reasons. If you are a housewife with three kids and your husband is the sole provider, what options do you have? That is at least the thought processes of people who are financially trapped. However, we did it without them at one point, and we will do it again!

The abuser made you feel like you are financially and familiarly trapped. They probably even set it up that way! That abuser might have told his housewife that she could quit her job or drop out of college, knowing very well that by doing so, she would be completely dependent on him.

Why Your Bond with Your Abuser Is Difficult to Break

This bond is difficult to break because you were conditioned not to break it! They told you that if you left, you wouldn't survive. As humans, we are trying to survive every day. Our heart beats while we sleep, we fight for air when we can't breathe. So when we think that we won't survive if we leave, then we are forced to stay.

How to Defeat the Narcissist

Before we continue, you should be very aware of the narcissistic supply and injury. The supply is everything that is given to a narcissist that they need in terms of approval, admiration, attention, and other things that feed their ego. As the codependent or empath responsible for providing these things, you yourself can be the narcissistic supply.

The injury, then, is when you are hurting the false self that the narcissist created. Anytime that you can take that supply away, then you are causing a narcissistic injury. Throughout the rest of this chapter, we are going to talk about all the ways that you can create that injury.

It sounds harsh, but they are the ones that have been hurting us for so long. At the end of the day, whenever you're combating a narcissist, you aren't hurting that person—you are hurting their false self. You are breaking down those walls that caused you to hurt so much in the first place.

Some people might be able to break away from that false self, and can follow their own path of recovery toward a place of healing. Others won't be so lucky and will stay in that fantasy place they have created their entire lives. Please note that your job isn't to heal the narcissist. That's what we need to remember throughout the rest of the book. Whether or not it's even possible is still up for debate by psychologists, and narcissists that have claimed to be completely healed are still under question by some professionals.

Regardless of what the truth is, the only thing you are responsible for is healing yourself. Trying to heal this other damaged person—the narcissist—might have been what got you to this stage of constant abuse!

How to Understand the Playing Field That Narcissists Thrive On

Narcissists are all about interacting. They are mostly concerned with making sure that they are in control of the interaction and that it goes their way. Through these interactions, whether they're talking to you, you're texting them, or even if they are actively ignoring you, this is how they get what they want.

To figure out how to best avoid this interaction or become aware of it when it is happening, you have to understand the playing field that they thrive on. Their game is to make sure that they preserve their false self. They will do whatever they have to in order to keep that illusion they created afloat. It doesn't matter who they hurt, if they're embarrassing themselves, or if they caused more damage than good in the end. When we understand that a narcissist only cares about protecting the image they created, then it will become much easier to beat them at their own game.

In order to preserve themselves (or this false self that they created, rather), they are going to go through phases where they are either building themselves up, making themselves seem like the most amazing person, or even showing their vulnerability (being too emotional and "weak") so that you are forced to take care of them.

A narcissist is like a child that built a treehouse with a piece of paper that says, "No boys/girls allowed." They built this imaginary safe space, the tree house, that they can escape to, keeping out things out that they don't want to have to deal with. They will go there whenever they are scared. If they ever get the sense that their treehouse is under attack (the treehouse representing their false self), then they are going to fight back twice as hard. They will have that childlike tendency when they fight as well. They don't care about hurting you, so they are going to come up with the most damaging things that they can think to say.

We forget that these narcissists don't fully care about our feelings. They make us think they are so loving in that first phase, that when they can say such hurtful things, we believe them. How can a person who tells you how much they love you and express their feelings creatively and movingly also tell you that you are the dumbest person they have ever met?

How can someone go from telling you that they want to share a family with you and grow old with you, to telling you that they wished they had never met you?

This is all part of their game. They know that they need to act this way to keep us around. Neither part of what they say is true— whether they hate or love us — because they are only capable of feeling anything for themselves. We latch onto those good things, and we want them to be true. The only way for them to be true, however, is if the bad stuff is also real — meaning, we also believe it when they say we have no value. Their goal is to make sure that their idolized self is preserved and they are going to do absolutely anything to make sure they reach it, whether it's telling you that you're worth nothing or everything.

How to Stop Playing Their Game

You are a piece in their puzzle, a chess piece in the match. Personally, this part was challenging for me to accept in my recovery — that I was just a tool. I thought back on the nights that we would be lying in bed together, discussing our hopes and dreams, sharing fears, and physically connecting.

Then I would remember the times when he would yell at me, make fun of my family, and try to isolate me from my friends. I would think to myself, "He's just a narcissist. He can't help it," when the bad stuff would happen.

But when the good things were happening, I didn't want to think the same thing. However, you have to accept that they are a sick person taking advantage of you in an attempt to feel better about themselves. I didn't want to have to believe this, but it was true, and once I accepted that, I started to feel better.

We have to stop playing the game by leaving. That's really all there is to it. Removal is the only way to stop the game. There is no winning of the game even when it ends. You both will still end up hurt. You can't win this game no matter how hard you try!

The narcissist is controlling everything, and they are going to make sure that they are the one on top when all is said and done. They will do what they have to in order to win, even if that means completely changing the game! The sooner we accept this, the easier it will be to move on. The only option you have is to leave. You can't keep playing a game that was set up to keep you trapped.

How to Confront a Narcissist in Their Behavior

It's important to remember one thing before we go forward with the rest of the book. If your abuser has displayed physical violence, then you should not attempt to leave on your own. It doesn't matter if it's your mom, sister, best friend, neighbor, or whoever. You do not want to put yourself in a situation where you're likely to get hurt.

If they have hit you at least once, do your best to avoid them altogether even if it means having someone else go and pick up your items. Likewise, if they've never laid a finger on you but have still displayed aggression, it's important that you use extreme caution.

It's going to be challenging to leave no matter what the situation is, but if physical abuse is involved, you don't want to risk your safety and should absolutely have someone with you. It will always be better to have a friend with you in all situations, but for physical abuse, it is a requirement.

When confronting the narcissist, the first rule is not to use your emotions when responding. This is going to be the hardest. How can you not show emotions with a person whom you developed an emotional connection with?

Unfortunately, if you are displaying too many of your emotions, then the abuser will have more they can tug at and use against you. No matter what they might be saying, it's important that you focus on staying calm and collected. You can tell them your opinion or share your emotions, but do not try to reason with them. Do not let them make you feel like your emotions aren't valid ever again.

If you want to talk with them for closure purposes, remember that they are not going to reason with you, especially if you are talking about yourself. Simply stay silent if you have to. When leaving them in a situation where you might have to move, don't engage when packing your stuff.

If you do, remember to stay calm and collected. Act as you would if you were a cashier dealing with a difficult customer. You might want to fight back and yell at them, but your manager is watching, so you have to kill them with kindness. This is how you have to interact with the abuser.

Next, make sure that you never apologize. Even if you might have said hurtful things back to them in the past, don't spend time apologizing, because chances are, you've already apologized enough. By not showing that you are sorry, your abuser will start getting the idea that you are aware of what's going on as well and that, this time, you are serious about actually leaving them and never coming back.

Make sure that you don't agree with them either. If they are saying, "You can't do that. This is messed up!" don't respond with "I know it's not right to leave you like this" or anything like that. You don't want to take any more responsibility for the dissolve of the relationship. It is not your fault that you have to leave. They are the ones that pushed you away. They were the ones that manipulated you.

It is going to be hard to interact with them. They are going to do what they can to hold on to you. They will take their last chance to try to get you back. They'll say, "I've been a terrible person in our entire relationship. I am aware that I have abused you, so I am going to work on myself so that I never hurt you again."

You shouldn't believe even a statement as big as this one! If they are serious, then make them show it. Move away and maybe try going on a date after a year of them proving that they have been in therapy and even rehab. Revisiting your abuser will be challenging, but you won't have to, because they won't change! They're just saying that because they want you to stay.

Make sure that you keep the conversations with the abuser very boring going forward. Don't give into anything they say. When they make a comment about you, nod and say "Okay." Find blanket terms that you might use for your boss or a colleague that you have a professional relationship with. Say simple phrases like "That's interesting," rather than engaging in conversation.

This is how your abuser is going to stop poking at you. They will notice that you are not giving any of the emotions that they're trying to evoke. Instead, you are focused only on making sure that you don't fall back into their traps.

You might have the urge to confront the narcissist at other times, maybe when they're in a good mood or being nice. You might think that maybe they've changed and that you could have an honest conversation with them about their behavior. But remember that this is common. If you are dull with the narcissist and don't give into their behavior after a week of engaging with them, you might notice that they start acting better. In a moment of weakness, you might think that it's okay to try and mend the relationship.

But do not fall into this trap. The narcissist will fall back into their cycle immediately. It took them years to form this personality disorder, and it's going to take just as long to get out of it. Maybe in years down the road, you could go back and talk to your narcissist about their behavior, but unfortunately, right now, there is no reasoning. They won't listen. The only interaction you should have with them is the one necessary for your survival; what you might need to do until you can make an escape.

Facing Difficult Encounters with a Narcissist

You have to remember that at this point, you won't be able to "win" with the narcissist anymore. Hence, you shouldn't try to fight them back. This isn't the answer most victims want.

You would like a perfect phrase to come up with, maybe something smart or snarky that you could say back to the abuser. But this isn't going to help the situation. It's only going to give them more ammo. They're going to use your words as fuel and find a way to use it against you. Remember that narcissists didn't get that way overnight. It took years of them conditioning themselves to think the way that they do.

After finishing this book, you might feel empowered, especially to the point where you think you're ready to confront your attacker. Remember that how you feel now is going to be a lot different than when you're back in front of them. In my own personal experience of having been in a narcissistic relationship, I had plenty of moments of feeling strong, thinking that it was time to tell my abuser, once and for all, everything he had done to me and how I wasn't going to take his abuse anymore. What would always end up happening was that we would get into a fight, and he would use the same manipulation tactics to make me think I was crazy. Then I would end up apologizing! He would make me feel guilty and shameful all over again.

Building strength takes time, and at first, you might not be as prepared as you think you are. The best option for you is to stay silent, submissive, and not give into a fight. This is what's going to hurt the abuser the most.

When they say mean things like, "What's wrong with you?" then they're looking for a fight. They want you to defend yourself so that they can hurt you even more by belittling your rebuttal. If you simply shrug your shoulders or shake your head, that's what's really going to bother them the most. Not reacting is a way to protect yourself while also making your abuser feel powerless in the struggle. You need to put an emphasis on making sure that you are protecting yourself. If they are threatening physical violence, you don't want to mock them or shrug them off. Do what you can to make sure that you can make it through the end of the interaction with as little harm as possible.

Obviously, the end goal is to stay away from them, but that's not going to happen overnight. If you are living in California with your narcissistic spouse, and everyone you know and love is in Maine, unfortunately, you might have to stay with them for a week or a few days to get things together and make arrangements. If you have children, then there will be times when you see each other for the kids' sake. We want to make sure that you are leaving your abuser, if you absolutely must interact with them, the next section will show you how to handle their attacks.

Handling Their Attacks

Remember to not grab the bait. A narcissist is going to put things out there for you to argue or fight about, but you can't latch onto it. When they notice that you're not reacting very much, they'll try to push you even further. They'll say all kinds of provocative things in hopes that they will be able to elicit a response to feed their ego.

They might want to start a fight directly as a result of something that you did, or perhaps they were having a bad day and needed to take it out on you. Either way, you have to stay calm and collected, and ignore them. When you give in, apologize, or try to defend yourself, you're giving them exactly what they want. The person who is going to come out the best in the situation is the one who stays silent. Though you are feeling emotions, do not act on them.

For times that your narcissist is really pushing you to give in and you haven't, sometimes, you may have to give in for a moment just to get them to stop. They can be relentless. But never place yourself in a harmful situation. If they don't seem to stop nagging you, simply bring up another conversation that involves them, and you will be surprised to see that they are often happy to start talking about themselves again. Think of topics that you could change the conversation to, like asking them about the rest of their day.

Alternatively, if they are really picking a fight and won't stop, then simply ask questions. Never apologize. If you do, then they will move on from the fight and start playing on your emotions. Even though you will be aware of what they are doing, it can still trigger you, potentially putting you back into a place where you have grown too fearful of leaving them.

If they are forcing you into an argument, tell them that you understand. When they're annoyed, don't respond with, "Okay, I'm sorry." Instead, say something like, "I understand. Is there something I can do to help you feel better about this situation?" When you throw the argument back at them and cause them to reflect, then that can be enough to silence them. If they are looking for an apology, that is for you to decide. You might want to give in to fear and apologize, and that's okay. Don't make yourself feel bad about it. Do your best to be resilient, but if you're afraid of physical abuse, obviously, you may have to give in to protect yourself.

In a normal, healthy relationship, people will bicker, argue, and even fight. They do so because they want to express their feelings, and fights can happen when the other person isn't being understanding. In a healthy relationship, however, there should be a period of reflection and apology, and it can help both parties grow.

A narcissist doesn't look at fighting like this. They simply want to prove their point for you to agree with them. They aren't fighting with you because they want to build character. They have confusing and unmanaged emotions, and they are going to take them out on you.

If you want to grow together in a normal relationship, then you will naturally have a desire to work things out, but you have to remind yourself that this is not going to happen with a narcissist. They will only use the argument as a way to try to validate themselves and how they are feeling.

How to Protect Yourself in the Company of a Narcissist

Cutting off contact is going to be the goal, but remember that there are some situations where cutting off contact is not possible. The narcissist might be your mother, father, or a sibling; and they will be in your life in times that you don't want but can't prevent. It's important that you are fully equipped to protect yourself in the company of a narcissist.

The first step you want to take is making sure that you aren't spending time with them alone. If it's a friend, a family member, or whoever else, do your best to make sure that they aren't around you and that you don't have to be alone with them. If it's your boss, when you have meetings, ask a coworker to go with you. The narcissist won't be manipulative in front of another person, and if they are, then you won't fall victim because the other person will be there to back you up.

Make sure that you are also careful with who you are bringing around the narcissist as well. If they are suspecting that you took their supply away from them, then they are on the prowl for their next victim. If you have to, suggest monitored visits when they are with your children. Make sure that if your kids are alone with the other narcissistic parent, you are giving them the tools to be powerful and stand up for themselves if needed. Narcissists are born from a lack of empathy, so fill your children or the other developing minds around the narcissist with empathy. Show them that they are loved.

Be cordial around your narcissist. They might ask to talk to you alone if you're at a party together, but don't allow this. They just want their chance to try to manipulate you and tell you things that they don't want other people to hear. When you can't establish no contact ever again (NCEA), then it is important that you are staying strong, reminding yourself of your worth, and not letting them hoover you.

Most of the time, if you stop giving a narcissist their supply, they will eventually leave on their own. They will either get bored with you, do everything in their power to hoover you, or in some rare circumstances, self-reflect and realize what they have done. What's most important for you is to stop giving into their narcissistic tendencies.

The Best Defense Mechanisms against a Narcissist

The best defense mechanisms that you will be able to use against a narcissist is your own voice. The first thing that you can do when confronted with a narcissist is to let them know that you understand how they feel. When you are open with a narcissist, no matter how irrational they are, and you talk about them, then there won't be much you can do to retaliate.

After that, make sure that you are talking in "we" and "us" terms. If you start pointing a finger and saying, "You did this," or "You did that," the narcissist is going to feel attacked. Instead, say something like, "We both have trouble properly communicating," or whatever else you're trying to point out in them, but with "we" statements.

Breaking Up With Your Narcissist

NCEA stands for "no contact ever again." This is the best method to use against a narcissistic abuser. It is also going to be the hardest. They were there for so long and have been such a part of your life that it seems crazy to think that you should just cut them out. Unfortunately, it's necessary and absolutely the best thing you can do for yourself.

There have probably been other people in your life that you didn't like and have had arguments with. What differs about the regular person that you butt heads with is that they are reasonable. You can discuss the argument with them and move past it toward a happier, healthier place for both of you.

The narcissist won't be so easily swayed. Sometimes (in most cases actually), the best thing that you can possibly do is to establish NCEA. This won't be entirely possible for those that have family ties, but for everyone else, this is what you should strive for. The hardest part is leaving the original idea of the person that you formed in your mind when you first met. You miss their false self, the one that was kind, funny, and sweet. Moving forward, you have to remember that their false self will not come back, and instead, you need to separate so that you don't fall back into cycles of abuse.

What you will have to do first is set boundaries of what you will have to do after no contact has been established. If you're young, not married, and don't have any kids, then your boundary should simply be to block them. However, if there be factors, such as children involved, then you have to decide how this will happen. Is there a family member that can pick up the kids to drop them off at your place or theirs? Will you be able to easily have full custody? Figure out your boundaries of contact and what those will be later on before you come up with your plan.

Next, you will want to find an escape plan for at least a month. If you already have your own apartment and are financially independent, this is going to be a lot easier. However, if you don't have work, they give you all the money, and you don't have a home, you will have to find a place to stay. If you don't have friends or family members, look into shelters for abuse victims. They might seem like scary places, but many will have resources, such as food donations and job support, to get you on your feet.

Afterward, determine what you'll do for money. This part will scare a lot of people as well. You might start looking at the cost of living and realize the rent and expenses of certain places, and get spooked into staying with the abuser. Remember that no agony as painful as what you've experienced with the abuser awaits you. Yes, there are some days where you wish you still had their income or the home you shared together. You will have moments when you want to go back because they were security. But you don't need that anymore. No sense of security is worth what they put you through.

Finally, it's time for you to cut every last tie with the other person. Delete and block their number. Change your phone number if you have to. Block them on social media, in your email, and everywhere else that they can contact you. Never share your personal information with them moving forward. And don't tell them where you live.

If they know where you live, you might consider staying with a friend for a while or having different friends stay with you so that you don't have to worry about being alone with them, should they find you.

If you are divorcing them, remember that this is a lengthy process. You don't have to know everything about how divorce works right away. Separation is going to be the most important part.

Points to Read When Feeling Irresolute on the NCEA Rule

The statements that we emphasized in the last chapter are going to be important for you to remember throughout this period. You went through something challenging — abuse that was malevolent, subcutaneous, and ingrained into your brain. You were conditioned and trained, and it's now time prevent something like this from ever happening again. Here are some important affirmations to remember should you want to give up and go back to the abuser:

1.   "I do not deserve what they put me through."
2.   "Wanting to go back is a response to the fear they created in me."
3.   "I am in control over my life, and no one has the power to tell me what to do."
4.   "I am stronger than my abuser's worst words."
5.   "I am only focused on protecting myself moving forward."

Dealing with Narcissistic Family Members

You can choose who you are friends with or whom you date, but you have no say when it comes to the family your born into. Unfortunately, having a narcissistic family member can be just as challenging to deal with as any other type of relationship—only in this situation, it's going to be almost impossible to establish NCEA.

The best method to deal with family members who are exhibiting narcissistic tendencies is to establish a contract together of when you are going to allow contact and when you feel it is important to keep yourselves separated. It doesn't have to be something that you write down and both sign; it can be something that both of you can to talk about together. You should limit the amount of the contact you're going to allow from them as well. Can they call you, text you, email you? Can they come to your home? You need to sit down and establish this relationship with the narcissist.

At first, they might think that your contract is absurd. Let them think whatever they want about it, but make it known that you need to establish this relationship for yourself. At the same time, you will also need to lay out the rules for how the two of you are allowed to connect. For example, you might state that if they start yelling at you, you will end contact immediately. If they raise their voice at you, then you will walk away.

Stay strict with this as well. Don't try to fight back. If they yell, call you names, gaslight, or do anything else that is part of their narcissistic character, then they are "in breach of contract," and you have the right to cut them off from contact.

Narcissism in Friendships

Although we might not see that person as often as we would a family member or romantic partner, narcissistic friendships can still be challenging. They can be just as damaging, and we need to come up with methods of protecting ourselves against them.

What can be frustrating about friendships is how we might have other friends in our circle that don't see the abuser for what they are. Instead, they might see them as normal people while you know that they have been narcissistically abusive toward you. It will not be up to you to change the way your friends see the narcissist. You just need to focus on protecting yourself against them in whatever situations you find the two of you in.

Your first step will be to talk to them about this

narcissistic behavior as it happens. When the two of you are hanging out, point it out when they say something mean or belittling. If they are willing to listen to you and open up about it, then that might mean your relationship is salvageable. If they get defensive and offended, they are still not in a place to talk, so cutting them out might be something to consider with this particular friend.

Workplace Narcissism

Narcissism in the workplace is hard because we try our best to keep emotions out of work as it is. What you have to remember first and foremost about workplace narcissism is that the other person isn't likely to change. They will be stuck in their ways, and trying to have a "therapy" session with them or getting them to confront their issues isn't going to be helpful.

Instead, you will have to find ways to work around them. Avoid joining team projects when you can, but if this isn't possible, make sure that you are working with them, not against them. If they are being bossy, don't tell them that. Instead, suggest that maybe they listen to others' suggestions, or try convincing them to share the tasks at hand.

You might want to beat them at their own game as well. When they are narcissistic, display the same behavior toward them. Don't ask them about their day or check on their emotions because they are not going to do the same thing for you.

Societal and Cultural Narcissism

Societal narcissism is all around us. After surviving personal abuse from a narcissist, it can be challenging to be immersed in a world that seems so oriented with themselves. You have to remember that you can't change any narcissist that you deal with, let alone society. The only thing you can do is be mindful of who you are interacting with. You have to learn how to stand up for yourself and remark when someone might have talked over you, belittled you, or shamed you in any way.

You also have to make sure that you're not always looking at everything through the lens of an abuse survivor. It can be very easy to become triggered by the situations you end up in. Don't let this get to you and set you back. Identify your triggers and come up with ways to diffuse.

Narcissistic Mothers, Fathers, or Siblings

Having a narcissistic mother, father, or sibling is never easy. Children can often be made to feel very bad about themselves, thinking that they were never good enough. Narcissistic family members will breed more narcissists, but for those who do have empathy, they might feel as though their spirits have been broken throughout their childhood.

Narcissistic families are founded on secrets. They will not be as willing to share personal information about their lives and events as other families. Growing up in a narcissistic family might have caused you to internalize a lot of the issues that are harder to talk about, like your emotions.

Narcissistic family members are also very concerned with how they appear to others. You were probably often told that you embarrassed them or didn't look good enough when out in public with them.

They will often give you feel negative about yourself, and this can be the hardest thing to grow from. If your mother constantly told you that you aren't beautiful enough or your father is always questioning your intelligence, then you are going to have those voices in your head, reminding you of what they would say in a situation even when they aren't there.

Your narcissistic family might have also made it difficult for you to communicate at all, not just about your emotions. They create an environment where you aren't allowed to be yourself, let alone express yourself, so that will be challenging moving forward.

When it comes to recovering from this, make sure that you are sharing your experiences with those you are close with. Let your romantic partner or best friends know that you might have narcissistic tendencies or that you are easily triggered by anger, violence, and manipulation. This is important because they can help you when you are feeling triggered, and will validate and let you know that they are only there to help, not hurt you.

The best way to handle your family is to avoid them if they are not willing to change. It can be hard, but you can't change other people, even if they're blood relatives. If they are more open and accepting of what damage they might have caused, then you can try to work through your issues and mend your relationship. This is when you might establish a contract with them. They might still have narcissistic tendencies even after they've admitted their wrongdoings and started healing, but you don't have to be responsible for their recovery. You only need to be concerned with how you are going to mend your own wounds moving forward.

Narcissistic Children

If you are a parent, you might start to worry that your children are displaying narcissistic tendencies. If they are young adults, then you would handle them the same way that you would an adult with narcissism. However, if they are younger and their behavior is concerning, then there are things that you can do to help.

First, look at the other parent to see if they are involved. If they are a narcissist, abusive, or neglectful, then this could have an impact on the way your child is behaving. While you might not be able to keep them away from the other parent, you can give them the tools necessary to build confidence in case they are picking up narcissistic traits from others.

Teach your children how to relate to others. Always point out how other people might be feeling. The more you can talk about your emotions with them and give examples of what those look like, the easier it will be for your child to understand their feelings and move forward. A narcissist lacks empathy, so if you can emphasize building this in your child, then they will be far less likely to develop NPD.

The Road to Healing and Restoration

Healing can be so challenging for those recovering from narcissistic abuse because the heart won't always listen to what the mind has to say. Instead, it will be torn apart, causing you to feel incredibly confused most of the time. It's like they are going in the completely opposite direction, and it's up to you to try to align them so that they are going in the same place.

A part of you may be saying, "I love them so much. I'll be nothing without them. They hurt me, but it is only because they have also been hurt themselves!" Then the other part of you is saying, "Get out of here ASAP!" It can be the hardest thing you'll ever do when you decide that it is over and you need to move on from your abuser.

Partly, you're also confused because your abuser has put those ideas in your head in the first place. They are the ones telling you that you need or won't be able to survive without them. As you go down this road to healing and restoration, it's important to remember that they're wrong and you're completely capable of doing this.

Becoming Aware of Narcissistic Abuse Damage

You need to become aware of the damage narcissistic abuse has done to your psyche to heal it. You probably know by now that your abuser is responsible for breaking down your self-esteem, telling you on multiple occasions that you are not good enough and always making you feel unworthy. Unfortunately, there are many other things that an abuser can do to you, and you might not even realize you were abused in the first place.

When you are first recovering, you are going to be looking at the "failures" of your life. You will become aware of the decisions that you made in the past that put you in the situation to be abused. You may think that it was your fault, and probably will feel regret and remorse, wishing you had done something differently so that your abuser would not have had much control over you as they did.

Always remember that this is simply your abuser talking. Sure, you might have made some decisions in the past that could have steered you elsewhere, but you could have still ended up with a different abuser or that person anyways. We can't look back on our lives and wish for things to have gone down differently. That is only going to make it harder to move forward.

Everything that happened is in the past, and there's no changing it.

It happened to you, and it was rough, but you made it through. Because of that, you are a stronger person now. Regret, guilt, and shame are all things that your abuser planted into your head. The more you can separate yourself from this kind of thinking, the easier it is going to be to heal yourself.

Once you have separated yourself from the narcissist or were fortunate enough for them to leave you, it's possible to go back to what they said was wrong with you. They might have told you that you were selfish at one point. Though being separated from them has helped clear your head, you might still think about the things they've said, wondering if there is any truth in them. Rather than focusing on what your abuser had done, you might cling to their words, wondering if they were right about you after all.

Again, remember that this is your abuser talking. They did everything in their power to pry open your brain and get you thinking like them, focused only on the thoughts that they have. Each time you start to think about your abuser, it's important that you turn that around and get any thoughts of them out of your mind.

Afterward, you may think about your abuser often and wonder if they are angry with you, thinking about you, or if you might have made a mistake. You might get the urge to go onto their social media pages, seeing what they are up to. They might even find a way to get in contact with you even after you blocked them, and try to start communication again. Remember that this is just your brain going back to this comfortable cycle. You were in a habitual relationship with them, so it's going to take a lot of time to break this pattern.

You also have to be aware of how you are going to think of them months or years down the line. You might start to wonder how they are doing, if they are a better person now, or if they have healed themselves. You might find yourself lost in nostalgia, thinking only of the good times and forgetful all the terrible things that they have done. Even if you've been separated for months, it can still be hard to push the thought of them out of your head.

Again, remember that this is still their lingering abuse, and it's a natural pattern for your brain to go back to them. You have to resist the urge to fall back into it as much as possible.

Among these things, there are other symptoms you may still suffer from as you recover. You are going to have constant memories and other intrusive thoughts that pop into your brain when you least expect. There will be moments when the last thing you want to think about is your abuser, but unfortunately, you won't be able to get them out of your head.

You might be confronted with some trauma as well. If a person is yelling or even manipulating someone, that could trigger you. If you are witnessing abuse on TV, it can be just as traumatizing for you as a real-life situation.

There could even be moments when you have flashbacks and nightmares, reliving the trauma to a degree where it feels like it is happening over again. You might start to notice that you are dissociating in other situations and avoiding certain things because of these challenging thoughts and feelings.

Your overall perspective might be damaged. You could be feeling bad about yourself and even worse about the world. Part of this might be the fact that their perceptions have altered yours.

Traditional Healing Methods

Going forward, focus only on healing. There are many different methods you can implement, but you have to be geared toward a healing mindset. This means that you understand that the thoughts you have of your abuser are a symptom of your abuse, not the truth, not a fact, and not just the way that things are.

You spent so much time trying to please the narcissist and do everything in your power to make sure that they were happy that you completely overlooked your own feelings and forgot to take care of yourself along the way.

It can feel strange now, as a recovering abuse victim, to put yourself first. You are going to feel bad for your abuser and guilty, wondering if they are going to hurt even more now that you left them. Remember that you are out of that dark place now, and you need to keep your head straight and focused on your own health.

Acknowledging the truth is going to be the most important part of the healing process. Sometimes people will start to say things like, "Well, I don't know if it really qualifies as abuse," way after the fact. Other individuals might start saying things like, "I don't really think that it was as bad as I remembered." You can't let yourself do this. What you experienced was real, and you need to acknowledge the truth. Trying to change reality after it happened is something that your abuser tried to do to you, so you can't do it to yourself. You need to focus only on moving forward.

Next, you need to put a great emphasis on forgiving yourself. A huge part of recovery is regret, wishing you hadn't done it in the first place. But remember that you didn't do anything. Your abuser told you that you did. They made you feel as though it was all your fault. They were the one that told you that this was happening because of you. Feeling regretful is just another symptom of the abuse you went through.

Forgive yourself. Know that it happened. Accept that it did and prepare to move forward. They were a toxic person, and they made it their mission to bring you down with them. It is not your fault, and it never will be. You were put through something that others will never survive, and it was not your fault.

You will need to have love and compassion for yourself moving forward. When you have thoughts about your abuser, don't punish yourself. Don't make yourself feel bad and say that you don't have worth. This is exactly what your abuser would have done. Instead, fill yourself with empathy and make sure that you love who you are and the person that you have become.

Now that you know how to get into the right mindset when it comes to going down the road to recovery, we are going to discuss some of the most traditional methods that abuse victims can follow in terms of getting help from others. Throughout these methods, you will find that you can change your own mental conditioning so that you are immune to their tactics.

CBT

CBT refers to cognitive behavioral therapy. It is a practice that emerged in the '60s and is a new approach to the way that we treat mental illness. It is a talk therapy that requires you to look at the cognitive distortions present and figure out how to turn them around. A lot of therapy is about going back to your roots, childhood, upbringing, and looking at the things that happened as a way to pinpoint what it might have caused now.

While this is important in recovery, CBT focuses instead on what is happening at the moment and how you are responding to the things that are going on around you. When presented with a stressor, we have certain reactions, and CBT will help us point those out and turn them around so that we don't have to worry about having these toxic reactions anymore.

CBT is traditionally done with a professional, but there are individuals that have made the best use of it on their own. The first major part of CBT is making sure that you change your perspective. Our brains are wired differently with various chemicals and neurons ready for response. After experiencing consistent abuse, your brain has certainly been wired a certain way, and now it's time to unravel that and turn it around in a direction that is more beneficial to your recovery.

When you are experiencing thoughts of your abuser, feeling anxious, experiencing low self-esteem, or going through a period of depression, ask yourself what's causing these thoughts. Which emotions are you feeling that have led to where you are now? What are you thinking about that's causing these struggles?

CBT will always be about challenging your thoughts. Make sure you notice the things that trigger you, what's causing your anxiety to inflate, and moments that make you have low self-esteem. When you can look into this, study and unravel it. It will be much easier to get over that cognitive distortion and move forward.

Another part of CBT includes balancing your thoughts. You have to make sure that your thoughts are always in harmony. Sometimes, we feel so bad about ourselves that it alters our perspective. You might think that you are hideous, so you hide inside and don't go out in public. When in reality, you are a completely normal-looking person, and no one would expect you to hide away because of your looks alone.

There are two sides to our thoughts — our opinions and the truth. Most of the time, the truth will be in your mind, but it's buried deep behind your trauma, upbringing, and other experiences that aid in the wiring of your brain. Make sure that you are finding a balance in all things that pass through your head. When you're thinking, "I'm so dumb," remember all the times that you are smart. When you are feeling ugly, remember all the people that add beauty to your life.

In your mind, include what is needed to counteract the present thought that is giving you anxiety, feelings of panic, or depressive emotions. Throughout this entire process, it is important for those that are using CBT to be kind to themselves. We have to make sure that we are being patient and not rushing this process. If we do, it will only make things more challenging in the end.

Be prepared to have "relapses" or moments when you might want to go back to that abuser. If you expect it to be a completely smooth ride, then you are only setting yourself up for disappointment.

Another big part of CBT is keeping a journal. You should write down what your triggers are, your fears, and the thoughts that you have on a day-to-day basis. This works firstly because it gives you a medium to express your emotions. You have been taught by your abuser for so long how to suppress those emotions and were even made to feel guilty for having them.

Don't let yourself feel that way anymore. Instead, focus on journaling so that you can fully let out all the deep things you are feeling. Journaling will also aid in reflection. When you are having a good day, you can write that down and talk about how great it feels to be happy. Then when you're having a bad day, you can go back to that good entry and find ways to cheer yourself up and improve your mood for the better.

Meditation

Another important method of recovery that many people find help with is meditation and mindfulness. This is the process of clearing your brain, recharging your thoughts, and balancing your emotions so that you can start fresh. Oftentimes, you might have a thought pop into your head in the morning, and you don't even realize how it might be negatively affecting your entire day and into the night as you're trying to sleep. If you take some time to meditate, then you can clear your head and refocus on what is most important.

The first step to meditation is finding a comfortable spot. Whether it's on the floor or if you're using a yoga mat, it doesn't matter. The only thing that you need to focus on is your breathing. Feel your air enter your body and exit slowly.

After that, start by pushing out any thought that comes into your head. Thinking about work? Clear your mind again. Are you thinking about your abuser? Push that thought out. This is going to be a crucial part of meditation.

Remind yourself that the different emotions that come through your body are temporary. No matter how major they feel, they will fade at some point, and you will still be left as who you are.

If you want, you can even include chanting or guided meditation in your routine. Chanting affirmation is going to be helpful in reminding you of the important things as you move forward. Affirmations would include true statements that are empowering and lift your spirit. The phrases in chapter 7 were examples of affirmations.

- "No agony awaits me as painful as what I have experienced from my abuser."

- "No sense of security is worth what my abuser put me through."

You can also find a lot of guided meditation online. This might include videos and audio recordings of people stating affirmations and phrases that will help keep you focused and centered. Many of these recordings are free on YouTube. If you listen to them as you are falling asleep or relaxing, they can help you to feel better without you even realizing it at first.

DBT

DBT, also known as dialectical behavioral therapy, is helpful because it gathers all that we discussed with cognitive behavioral therapy and combines it with behavioral therapy. The goal is to make unhealthy patterns go away, along with the negative thought processes that come along with them. This is something that needs to be done with a professional but will help in your recovery.

What you will do throughout this therapy is regulate your emotions and figure out what you need to do to self-manage, reduce anxiety, and regulate your overall stress levels.

Support Groups

As someone suffering from abuse, especially a person who is codependent, it might feel unnatural to ask for help. On your road to recovery, it can be one of the most important things that you can do. A great method that will help you find the skills needed to keep moving forward is to find a support group of people that also suffered from narcissistic abuse.

When you can find a community of people like you, with individuals that know what you went through, it will be a lot easier to feel less alone throughout your recovery. You can share coping mechanisms, tips, fears, and other things that you want to express with others.

By surrounding yourself with people who understand what you're going through and are on this journey themselves, it will bring clarity to what your abuser did, who they really were, and the tactics they used to control you. If you can't locate a support group in your local community, there are lots of places online, like forums that you could find as well people you can reach out to.

Negative Childhood Programming Release

There are a lot of things that we went through as children that might have led us to become magnets for narcissists. While you aren't doing these things intentionally, they are what allowed you to stay in a narcissistic relationship even after you might have seen the warning signs. Again, never punish yourself for what has already happened. It is important to be aware of them so that you can change this behavior and protect yourself as you move forward.

Making excuses is a toxic pattern of thinking that can only hurt you. You might have done this often when you were with your abuser, always diminishing the damage they actually did with excuses for their behavior.

You need to make sure that you are letting others care for you, as well as show you love and compassion. If you are not allowing yourself to do this, then you are placing yourself back in that abusive cage, protecting yourself from outside sources.

Always be aware of red flags moving forward. You don't want to find yourself going through the same process again with another abuser, so be mindful of the things that an abusive person has that can make them so intrinsically damaging to your character.

Eliminating People-Pleasing Habits

One of the reasons why your abuser might have "picked" you is also because of your people-pleasing habits. Many individuals are self-described people pleasers, and there are plenty of others that aren't even aware of their behavior or how it could be hurting them. Recognize when you might have these issues.

The need to be a people-pleaser sometimes comes from insecurity, but mostly, people just want to have others around them and enjoy avoiding conflict. This is because of childhood conditioning, and it is also a survival technique for adults. While it can be helpful in some situations, maybe at work or with other formal social settings, in your everyday life, you can't please everyone.

The way that you will eradicate people-pleasing habits is to learn how to say "No." Tell them "No" when they are asking too much of you or when you feel like you are being pushed outside of your comfort zone. "No" is going to be one of the most important words you'll have moving forward.

You might be worried about what will happen if you start saying "No" more often. You will wonder if people will start leaving you or won't be as interested in building a relationship with you. If this happens, then so be it! If people aren't in your life now that you are standing up for yourself, then they probably only there to take advantage of you in the first place! It's always nice to be giving and generous with others, but not when you are sacrificing parts of yourself that you will never get back.

How to Restore Balance to Your Relationships

After the abuse has ended, you might find that you need to restore other relationships. Maybe your parents shut you out because you wouldn't leave your partner, or perhaps your partner left you because you weren't managing your unhealthy relationship with your parents properly. Whatever the case may be, it's important to recognize the hurt that other people have caused you and how you also might have hurt others in the process.

Now it is time for you to work on restoring the balance back to all your relationships. If you have to, ask them to come to therapy sessions with you. You might be afraid to reach out to them because of the way you left things, but don't let your abusive relationship ruin all the other important relationships in your life.

The same can be said about relationships moving forward. It can be hard to trust new partners that show a tiny sign of narcissism because it might only be a matter of time before they turn into the abusers you've dealt with in the past. If someone makes a joke about you, it can trigger thoughts that they're belittling you, but this is something you have to work through because, for the most part, the joke probably wasn't meant to be taken harshly. You only perceive it that way because your abuser spent so much time mocking you.

Don't let the last person bleed into the new relationship. It's not fair to assume that everyone will be the same. Don't be ignorant to red flags, but also remember that not everyone you meet is going to be a narcissistic abuser moving forward.

Disengaging from Manipulators

Not all manipulators are narcissistic abusers either. Some people will simply be in a dark place in their life and manipulate others as a result. When you recognize that manipulation is happening, you should point it out. Tell the other person that they are putting too much pressure on you, making you feel uncomfortable, or that you need more time to think about the decision.

Sorry to interrupt again, but...

Are you enjoying this book? If so, then I'd love to hear your thoughts!

As an independent author with a tiny marketing budget, I rely on readers, like you, to leave a short review on Amazon.

Even if it's just a sentence or two!

So if you enjoyed the book, please...

Visit www.**TitleRatings.com/narcissist** and leave a brief review.

I personally read every review. So be sure to leave me a little message.

I'd like to thank you from the bottom of my heart for purchasing this book and making it this far. And now, move on to the next page to the final chapter!

Personal Experiences with Narcissists

In this chapter, we're going to go over some real experiences with narcissists, what the victims learned, and how they were able to overcome this abuse. Listening to other people's stories can be encouraging to know that you aren't alone in your recovery.

Stories

"A great resource for codependents and HSPs alike..."
In a YouTube account titled Nu Mindframe, one user shares her story of narcissistic abuse, discussing how one toxic relationship left her feeling isolated, hopeless, and exhausted. In her case, she was a codependent as a result of the abuse that she experienced as a child. She states that the abuse took place because catering to the needs of her abusers was the way she survived.

Because of this, she would do the same thing in romantic relationships, making it the perfect narcissistic supply. Eventually, she ended up with a narcissistic partner. Blinded by the love-bombing phase, they would text for up to thirteen hours a day. During this phase, her abuser was taking in all the personal issues that she shared with him. He would agree with her and make her feel validated, while collecting information about her that he would eventually use in the devaluing phase.

Her story is a familiar one, and her channel is also a great resource for getting over these types of problems, along with other personal relationship issues. The specific narcissist abuse video is titled: "The 3 Stages of Narcissistic Abuse + My Experience."

Other Cases

"I'd rather be homeless than take any more of this abuse!"

Marci met an extremely charming man whom she fell for quickly. He lived close by and was readily available any time of day or night. Her journey into darkness began not long after they began dating. While out with friends they ran into an old girlfriend of his, and he proceeded to shower this woman with all his attention. When Marci left to go home, he followed her outside and violently slapped her. Of course, he was sorry later and vowed it would never happen again. But it did, over and over, even when she became pregnant with his child. Marci stayed, hoping the abuse would end, hoping he would stop drinking, hoping life would get better. After having three children, he began to abuse the children and Marci knew she needed to get out. It took staying several weeks in a homeless shelter and eventually moving to public housing in a new state, but eventually, Marci was able to move on.

"Aren't churchgoers supposed to be innocent?"
Jean met her narcissistic abuser at church. They dated for over a year before eventually marrying in the same church they met, surrounded by family and friends. The actual abuse began after the marriage. When Jean became totally fed up with the abuse and asked for a divorce, her husband told her he would kill her if she ever left. When she was able to get him to go to counseling, he told the minister a totally different story than what Jean knew to be true. Eventually, he began putting restrictions on her time away from home. One by one, he alienated Jean's family and friends. He continuously told Jean how worthless she was and how no one else would ever want her. He confused her so much that she began to think the problems were all her fault. One day Jean gathered the courage to call the police after one, particularly bad beating. The police helped her to leave and get to a battered woman's shelter. Jean eventually moved back home and rebuilt her life.

"Wait! I thought only men were narcissists."
Carla met her girlfriend and knew she was the one. The girlfriend was fun to be around, very romantic; a bit secretive at first but nothing worth mentioning. A few

months into the relationship, suddenly Carla wasn't exciting enough anymore. The girlfriend began talking about other women she was seeing and compared Carla to them. Then she began attacking Carla because she drove the "wrong car," wore the "wrong clothes," and enjoyed the "wrong movies." Carla found herself apologizing more often than not. The girlfriend was never physically abusive, but the mental and emotional abuse was enough to make Carla want out of the relationship. Carla even tried to do things the girlfriend's way for a while, spending more time drinking and pub crawling even though it really wasn't her scene. They would break up and make up almost immediately. This pattern continued until the day Carla realized she'd hit rock bottom. She broke up for the last time and turned to her mother and sister for help rebuilding her life, as they had never totally given up on her escaping from the girlfriend's evil clutches.

"She told her son she wished she never had children!"
Bob lived with a narcissistic mother for many years before he finally saw her for what she really was. One night she looked at him and said she wished she had never had children because they were the biggest drain on her mental well-being. After years of trying to please his mother, first as a child and then as a young man, Bob suddenly realized, in a moment of clarity, that the neglect he had suffered over his lifetime had

not been his fault at all. Bob was finally able to break free of his mother's manipulation and control. He no longer felt the need to try to win her love and approval, because he knew it would never happen. He also realized he would never be able to live up to her impossible standards because she kept raising the bar even higher. When he stopped trying to please his mother, he was able to begin living his life.

"Does the narcissist admit he was wrong?"
Although it's rare, sometimes the narcissist themselves can make a life-altering change. Clarke will be the first to admit he was once a narcissist. Clarke admits that his relationships operated the way he wanted them to. He always sought strong and well put together women who thought he was a great guy—until he started chasing a successful event at work or another gorgeous woman. He didn't care how much they might complain. His needs always came first. Clarke felt justified in acting the way he wanted; after all, it was his world that was most important. If the woman wasn't happy, she could leave. Some did, but more often Clarke got bored and left them first. He did feel bad about most of the breakups, but then just shrugged his shoulders and went on a pursuit to the next one.

Eventually, Clarke began to tire of the chase. As exciting as it was, he yearned for something deeper and more meaningful—something more like a real relationship that might last more than a few months. But Clarke knew he would first need to address the issues that were causing him to act the way he did, beginning with his overriding selfishness. With the help of a therapist, Clarke was able to identify patterns that made him narcissistic. Something he realized was that in a narcissistic relationship, one person would win while the other would lose. In order for both partners to win, he would need to learn to treat them as an equal and not a vessel for fulfilling his needs.

Clarke feels he has made progress but still has a ways to go before he can truly call himself cured. But he is enjoying the new life that freedom from narcissism has given him."

A First-Person Account

My situation is different from others. The cycle of my abuse started in my childhood. I grew up with a single mother who worked often, so my grandmother was my main caretaker. She was a narcissist who often inflated things and would always take offense to minor inconveniences. She would get upset often, and as a child, I would assume that I had done something wrong.

The way my grandmother acted, plus my mother's neglect, resulted in me forming codependent traits. The only way I could get attention in the household was when I was helping others or "serving" them in some way. I would listen to my grandmother's rants and do chores beyond my age to get praise from my working mom.

I grew up taking care of other people's needs first. I didn't have a way to express my feelings or emotions, so I would instead put the attention on how other people were feeling. If others were having a bad time, I would as well. When I could sense someone might be mad, I would get anxious. It didn't matter who it was — my mom, teacher, boss, friends. I was scared often, always wanting to make other people happy.

Then I met my first boyfriend, and everything felt right. He was so sweet to me, always making sure that I was happy. He would ask how my day was, get me to laugh and smile like no other, and would make me feel more loved than anyone else I could speak for at that time. Others would tell me I was glowing, and people would ask who it was that always had me smiling.

He love-bombed me as intensely as he could, and I loved it. This was also my first romantic relationship, and I hadn't seen any healthy ones growing up, so to me, this was perfection. I had found "the one." He would talk about having kids and how he wanted to take care of me in the early stages of our relationship. I didn't realize soon after, however, that he was just trying to charm me.

Eventually, the weight of the relationship started to shift. He would ask to hang out, and I couldn't, so he would "punish" me by not talking to me for days. Then when he would come back, he would love-bomb me again. This was so minor that I figured it was normal for some people to just respond to anger that way. I looked at it as giving him time to breathe. I didn't realize that he was actually isolating me, a narcissist tactic.

Eventually, not much charm was left, and he would even start to mock me. He would joke about a band I liked or a movie I watched. He would laugh so hard after that it would make it seem strange I wasn't laughing too. If I joked about him, he would roll his eyes and look away, something I would hardly do.

I would make us dinner, pay for it all myself, and spend time cooking; but he would ask for at least half of the cost when he would buy fast food or a frozen pizza.

Through it all, I didn't think much of it because I was a codependent person, and taking care of him was all I knew.

Then just a few days after we spent the holidays together, I found out that he was cheating on me with his ex-girlfriend and had a dating profile that said he was single. I was in shock but realized quickly he had probably been cheating on me the entire time. He was a serial cheater and covered it up with his narcissism. I fell for it because I wanted to. I liked caring for someone and being loved.

I got through it by remembering all the things I discussed throughout this book. I overcame even when I wanted to go back, forgive him, and start over. It wasn't easy, but my life is so much better now than with the years I spent with him.

Conclusion

I want to end this book with an uplifting and encouraging message for moving forward. For a long time, I would ask, "Why me? Why has this happened to me?" I would look at other people in normal and healthy relationships and wonder why I couldn't have one. I would feel so lonely, having nights when I would wonder if I should go back to my abuser. Before I even met him, I was scared and alone, desperately craved the attention of other people.

This wasn't easy to live with or admit once I discovered it. I would ask why I had to go through this struggle, what I might have done in my past that led to this. I would think this was my punishment for something I forgot I did. Then one day, throughout my recovery, I realized that I was content that I had experienced the abuse, because, without it, I wouldn't be the strong person I am today. I was still a codependent person from childhood, and had I not been in a toxic relationship, it could have taken me longer to figure it out, or I could have gone forever not confronting my past trauma.

I wouldn't say I'm glad it happened, because it was a very painful experience that can even be challenging now to recount. I can, however, say that I'm not completely upset that it happened. I could have learned similar lessons in different ways, but as I started to enjoy my life, it seemed like everything had fallen into place.

You might not be at that place yet, and that's okay. We all go through things that make us think the world is ending. The more challenges I had to confront, the more I realized that I was more fearful about what was going to happen. I was so scared to leave the abuser for a while, but once I actually did, it wasn't as scary as I thought. It was challenging, but I didn't experience the constant fear I thought I would. No matter how scared you might be now, it will be okay. Nothing as terrible will actually happen as what you are experiencing now.

When we have a child, we know that everything in our life happened perfectly, just as it should have. If we had done even one minor thing differently, then there's a chance we wouldn't have that child. The same can be said for when you meet your true love, find the perfect job, or do whatever else that makes you feel whole. When you can find an appreciation for life, a satisfaction with who you are, and an understanding of the good we must go through to get there, it can be easier to recover and find peace with our past.

The next step is to use the information found in this book to create a better life for yourself. If you are the narcissist, you should seek help to break the cycle of narcissistic abuse and learn how to develop relationships with others. If you are a victim, you can use the tips contained herein to help you improve your life, leave the victim mentality behind, and develop more meaningful relationships!

If you enjoyed Narcissist Abuse Recovery, then you'll love the previous book in the series called
Codependent Cure

If you're always giving away parts of yourself to others, even when it hurts, or are afraid of getting burnt in a relationship because you care too much, then this book will give you the knowledge to control codependent habits and eventually to get rid of it, so that you can begin to love yourself instead!

To check out this book, visit:
www.BonusGuides.com/codependent

References

Caligor, E., Levy, K. N., & Yeomans, F. E. (2015). Narcissistic personality disorder: diagnostic and clinical challenges. *American journal of psychiatry*, 172(5), 415–422.

Carlson, E. N., Vazire, S., & Oltmanns, T. F. (2011). You probably think this paper's about you: narcissists' perceptions of their personality and reputation. *Journal of personality and social psychology*, 101(1), 185–201. doi:10.1037/a0023781.

The American Psychiatric Association. (2019). DSM-5.

Jauk, E., Weigle, E., Lehmann, K., Benedek, M., & Neubauer, A. C. (2017). The relationship between grandiose and vulnerable (hypersensitive) narcissism. *Frontiers in psychology*, 8, 1600. doi:10.3389/fpsyg.2017.01600.

Kernis M. H., & Sun, C. Narcissism and reactions to interpersonal feedback. *Journal of research in personality*. 1994; 28:4–13.

Narcissistic personality disorder. Cleveland Clinic.
(2019). Retrieved from
https://my.clevelandclinic.org/health/diseases/9
742-narcissistic-personality-disorder.

Speaking of psychology: recognizing a narcissist.
(2019). Retrieved from
https://www.apa.org/research/action/speaking-
of-psychology/narcissism.

Stinson, F. S., Dawson, D. A., Goldstein, R. B., Chou, S.
P., Huang, B., Smith, S. M., Grant, B. F. (2008).
Prevalence, correlates, disability, and
comorbidity of DSM-IV narcissistic personality
disorder: results from the wave 2 national
epidemiologic survey on alcohol and related
conditions. *The journal of clinical psychiatry*,
69(7), 1033–1045.

Made in the USA
Las Vegas, NV
19 November 2023